A Bailey Island Girl *Remembers*

Janet Freeman Barbeau

PUBLISHED BY
Janet Freeman Baribeau

DESIGNED BY
Will-Dale Press

PHOTOGRAPHS BY
Cover Photo by my nephew, Donald Freeman
Back Cover Photo and July 4th 2010 Photo by my grandson, Zachary Sharpe

PRINTED BY
Will-Dale Press
Bowdoin, Maine

ISBN
978-0-615-48300-9

A
Bailey Island Girl
Remembers

JANET FREEMAN BARIBEAU

Acknowledgments

I am indebted to the following people for their contributions to this book:

To my husband Dennis – for his enduring patience and understanding of my determined obsession to write, rewrite and finally complete this book. He's gone through the whole frustrating process with me.

To my granddaughter Jessika Hyde – for writing her letter to me when she was ten years old requesting information on my early years and on our family history. This was the beginning of my quest!

To my editor Charles J. Martin – for providing me with the kind of constructive criticism, support and attention to detail that I was so desperately seeking.

To my six children – for always being there to encourage and spur me on when I was feeling frustrated and ready to quit.

To my brother Gordon – for helping our mother decide to buy me my first computer. I could never have done this without it!

To my sister Connie, Ercil White and Kerry Matteson, – for sharing their collections and family pictures, many of which appear in this book.

Acknowledgments

To Dale A. Woerter and KymNoelle Sposato at Will-Dale Press in Bowdoin, Maine – for designing and printing <u>A Bailey Island Girl Remembers</u>. It has been a relaxed and comfortable venture for this 72-year old author trying to self-publish her first book!

To Shea D. Mowat – for granting me permission to use his father's map of Orr's and Bailey Island.

To my childhood friend, Nancy Johnson Jensen – for loving Bailey Island as I do and for coming to Maine in 1999 to join me in the writing class that spawned this book as well as her first book, <u>Bailey Island – Memories, Pictures & Lore.</u>

To Phil and Holly Shea in Ellsworth, Maine – for sharing their family stories and for taking the time to show me where in Ellsworth the Shea family had lived, worked and were buried.

I can't begin to thank all those who have helped me with information that may appear in this book, but you all know who you are, and I do thank you! I've written all of the personal stories as honestly as my memory allowed, but there were areas where I had to fill in the blanks with the way I thought it would have been. Maintaining accuracy and consistency in recording dates, names, etc., has been a real challenge, and I apologize in advance for any discrepancies, omissions or errors.

Author's Notes

I've been writing this book, in one way or another, since the 1970s. It all began after I bought my first <u>OUR FAMILY HISTORY</u> book for recording family information. The beginning pages were easily filled in with the names and dates of births, deaths and marriages of our immediate families. Along with helping me gather bits and pieces of information about our Harpswell ancestry, my mother also shared her stories. I always loved those stories, and the more I knew about our ancestry the more curious I became!

With my limited information jotted down in a notebook I started visiting all the local cemeteries where I copied every name and date that pertained to our Harpswell ancestry. My next step took me to the Harpswell Town Office where the kind and helpful ladies sat me down with old record books to find whatever information I was searching for at the time. I went there many times, and after each visit I was able to fill in another missing piece of the puzzle.

Our Linscott ancestry has always been of great interest to me. This branch of our family tree was listed in the <u>First Settlers of Harpswell Prior to 1755</u>. I loved the stories of my great-great-grandmother Mamie Linscott's successes at midwifery, tending to the medical needs of her family and the community with her little black bag and no formal education. Mamie's husband Moses B. Linscott was also a colorful character. He and his brothers had a lucrative fishing business based on Little Island in the late 1800s.

Researching the Leeman family took me on another adventure to the Maine State Library. There I learned that a fifth-generation member of our family, Samuel Leeman, Jr., married Caroline Hall of Georgetown, Maine, in 1828. I also discovered <u>Cemetery Records</u> books for many towns in Maine at the Maine State Library. In one of the cemetery record books Caroline's parents were shown as being buried in the Hall-Beal Cemetery in Georgetown. Explicit directions and a map to the cemetery were provided. The Hall-Beal Cemetery is located on the east shore of the marsh at the head of Hall's Bay, but it was a bit of an adventure to find.

My cousin Ercil offered to join me on this little outing to find the Cemetery. Armed with my records, directions and map we drove towards Georgetown. We turned off onto the Robin Hood Road and then to the Flying Point Road where we stopped just before the marsh, parked our car and headed into the woods. Even though we faithfully followed the map and its directions we found ourselves getting farther and farther into the thick dark woods. Just when we were ready to turn around and start walking back to the car, we found it! There in the middle of the deep woods, almost totally hidden from view beneath the trees, bushes, leaves and ground cover, was the little family cemetery.

There were a number of unmarked fieldstones there as well as the markers of Caroline's father, mother and sister who all died at young ages in the first half of the 19th century. Her father William Hall died in 1828 at age 45. Her mother Mary (Goodwin) Hall died in 1810 at age 22, and her sister Martha, died in 1845 at age 38.

I have one more story that shows where genealogical research can sometimes take you if you are persistent. In the first chapter of this book you'll meet my great-grandmother Anna Sophia (Lorenzen) Doughty. When I first asked family members about this interesting little lady, all anyone could tell me was that at age sixteen she left Germany (although she always said she was Danish and not German) to travel alone to the United States with a black wooden box her father had built for her things.

The box that carried her possessions from Germany to America and a cardboard box of pictures from the old country were given to me some years ago. As you'll see when you read this chapter, Anna's full name as well as the name and address of the people she was going to live with in 1871 were still legible on the old black wooden box. She went to live with the George Boyson family.

Several years ago my brother Gordon and his wife Judy were about to leave on a trip to Germany. At the same time I was doing some research at the Maine State Library in Augusta, and I came across George Boyson's name in the Cambridge, Mass. VR to 1850. The record showed that he was born in Nieblum, Germany, November 29, 1839, and that his grave was in the Cambridge Cemetery on Coolidge Avenue.

I was convinced this had to be the George Boyson our great-grandmother Lorenzen had come to live with in Cambridge, Mass. I drove to my brother's house in Dresden that same afternoon with a folder that contained a photocopy of the George Boyson record and copies of related Lorenzen pictures from the cardboard box.

Gordon and Judy then departed for Germany, and a few days later they knocked on Ernst and Maria Lorenzen's door in Nieblum, Fohr. The Lorenzens were hesitant about letting these two strange Americans into their home until my brother showed them the pictures in the folder. When Ernst saw that one of the pictures was of him as a young man with two of his cousins, John and Henry Lorenzen, he was shocked and said, "That's me!" Instantly the door was opened to them, and it was the beginning of a reunion and connection with a branch of our family that we had known little or nothing about.

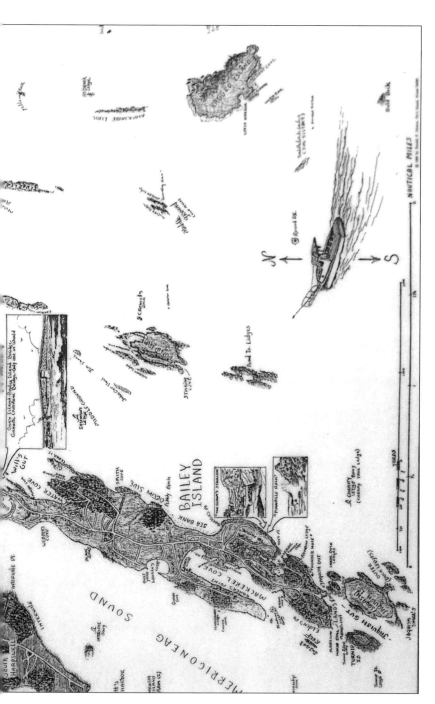

This wonderful Orr's and Bailey Island map was created in 1968 by my talented and artistic cousin Ronald F. Mowat.

Dedication

I'd like to dedicate *A BAILEY ISLAND GIRL REMEMBERS* to my dear mother, Celina Shea Freeman, who loved the Islands and who shared so many of its stories with me in her lifetime. I thank her for the wonderful gift of these stories.

My mother always enjoyed my writings and had faith that my book would one day be a reality. I'd hoped to have it written while she was alive to enjoy it, but sadly she passed away on February 2, 2002.

I know, however, that she is rejoicing that it is finally finished, and that it will always be there for her cherished family and for all those who loved the Islands, its people, and its ways, as she did.

Contents

Acknowledgments		4
Author's Notes		7
Orr's & Bailey Islands Map		10
Dedication		13
Granddaughter Jessie's Letter		16

CHAPTER		PAGE
1	Freeman Family in Maine	17
2	Our House at Bailey Island	27
3	World War II Years	33
4	Health & Dental Care	37
5	Bailey Island School	39
6	Growing Up on Bailey Island	47
7	Canning Season	57
8	Well in the Field	61
9	Cedar Island Beach	65
10	Clams, Razor Clams & Mussels	71
11	A Cold Night in January	75
12	Winter at the Farm	79
13	Pyrex Bowls & Creamed Toast	81
14	Great-Grandfather Elisha Leeman	85
	Grampy Leeman's Chocolate Cake	90
15	Lobstering with 'Lish Leeman	93
16	Favorite Holidays & Birthdays	97
17	Outer Islands	111
18	Orr's Island Grammar School	119
19	The Towers of World War II	131
20	Summer Jobs	135
21	Hattie E (Leeman) Shea	141

Contents

22	James Cotter Shea	155
23	Selina (Celina) Shea Freeman	163
24	Janet Freeman Meets Dennis Baribeau	179
25	Johnson – Leeman	183
26	Linscott – Shea	189
27	Lawrence Elwell Johnson	205
28	Edmund "Rip" Black	211
29	Phil Baker	213
30	Alfred Perry	217
31	KKK on Orr's & Bailey Islands	221
	The Ugly Head of the KKK	224
	by Philip Curran	
32	Joanne Johnson Lund	229
33	Prince's Store at Orr's Island	237
34	Mysterious Sinking of the Don	241
35	Brunswick Record Excerpts	251
36	My Scrapbook of the Islands	259
	References	274

9-11-96

Dear Memere,
      I love school so much. I have
Mrs. Ainsworth for homeroom and Mrs.
LaPierre for math. On the first day of
school we had homework. And yesterday we had two tests. We just finished a
book called Maniac Magee. It was cool.
      I can't wait until Aunt Joyce gets
married. Kaitie got to be junior brides
maid and Matt gets to be the best man.
They are so lucky. At first I was
jealous, but I got over it. We just got
our song on "Going to the" chapel
and we're gonna get married.
      So have you written any more
articles? I love your articles. I think
I want to be a writer when I get
older, because I like history. Actually,
that's why I'm writing to you. I need
you to write about your childhood.
      Here are some of the things I want
you to write. Oh yeah, it has to be
done as quickly as possible, because I
need the information for a book I'm
writing on our family history. I would like
to know about the embarrassing thing that
happened or when you fell in love. Maybe
you liked different subjects or mean teachers. Or did you work? Did you ever get
in trouble? If you did, what kinds of
punishments where there? And how did
you get to school.
      Thanks for trying to help me.
do a great job in school. My book will be great.
Well, got to go.

            ♡ Love, ♡
            ☺ Jessie ☺

Granddaughter Jessie Hyde's letter – thus began my first short memoir.

1
Freeman Family in Maine

T he day after Christmas 1938 was a stormy one. The wind howled and drifted the heavy snow up to the windows and doors of the old farm in the first nor'easter of the season. My father worked hard trying to keep his family warm that cold winter night. He tended the fires in the wood stoves and kept them well stoked with the dry, well-seasoned hardwood logs from the shed, but it was impossible to compete with the cold, bitter northeast wind. The cold seeped through the thin glass of the single-paned windows and the un-insulated walls and floors of the old farmhouse.

My grandmother, Hattie Shea, was staying at the farm for the holidays. She was there to help my mother and to be there when she went into labor. Afraid of the big snowstorm forecast on the radio that morning, Dad sent word to the doctor as soon as Mum started having pains, and Dr. Stetson got there ahead of the storm. Although it was a long hard labor, there were no complications. I presented myself on the day after Christmas . . . a healthy, robust long-awaited baby girl.

While the doctor cleaned me, my father weighed himself on the scale in the corner of the room, then held me for the very first time and stepped back onto the scale. I weighed over eight pounds. He held me close for a few minutes before putting me back into my mother's arms where I instantly rooted for her breast, making slurping, sucking sounds. Mum and Dad both looked at each other and smiled. As Mum's eyes got heavy and started to close, Dad kissed her and picked me up to lay me on Nanny Shea's chest where she was resting on a cot in the same room where my mother was finally able to sleep. Nanny cuddled and kept me warm beneath the woolen blankets and heavy patchwork quilt.

Above the bed where my mother had just given birth hung a very large picture of a majestic-looking lion in an ornately gilded frame. From my earliest memories and for all the years our family owned the farm, the lion picture hung there on the wall in the front room where it continued to witness the joys and sorrows of the Freeman family.

I was the second child in our family. My parents and four and a half year old brother, Philip Gordon, were spending the winter months of the year I was born at the Freeman Farm. During that time my father worked on lobster trap gear for the upcoming season, and our parents worked together in the woods of the Freeman Farm. They felled trees with a crosscut saw. My mother was on one end of the saw and my father on the other. After the trees were down and limbed, they used a bucksaw to cut the trees into four-foot lengths to sell. Selling wood brought in enough money to get them through the long, cold winter months. In the spring they would pack up and move back to the apartment in the other end of Grampy Leeman's house on Bailey Island.

Fifty years had passed since that cold winter night I was born, and once again it was the Christmas season. My youngest daughter Denice and I went to the farm to visit Aunt Shirley Freeman who had not been well. Bearing our gift of homemade banana bread, we made our way through the old shed at the back of the house. We stomped our feet, kicked the snow off our boots and climbed the well-worn steps up to the kitchen door. We knocked several times and waited, but no one called out or came to the door, so we lifted the latch and entered the big farmer's kitchen. The warmth and unmistakable scent of burning cedar was our only welcome.

I set the loaf of bread down on the big round heavy oak table that still stood, where it always had, in the middle of the big room. We listened for some sign of life in the old house as we warmed our hands over the kitchen stove. The only sound to be heard was the snap-crackle of the wood burning

Lorenzen family home on Lorenzwarft at Hallig Hooge – 1870s

in the Home Comfort range. Reluctantly we left the warm kitchen and walked through the middle room and on into the front room. Aunt Shirley was lying in a hospital bed there. She was in her final illness. There above her head hung the infamous lion picture still continuing its watch over the Freeman family.

My mother and I visited the farm several years before my mother's death in 2002. James and Mary Beth Ford had bought the farm and invited us for tea one afternoon. We shared stories and pictures of our family's time there and inquired about the lion picture. Mary Beth said it was in the house when they first moved in, but the picture was damaged beyond repair and ended up in their junk pile out in the barn.

I've always been curious about the lion picture and its significance. It seems there must be a family story there somewhere…

Anna Sophia Lorenzen

The year was 1871 when 16-year old Anna left her parents, brothers, sisters and the only home she'd ever known on the small island of Hallig Hooge in the North Sea. Times were hard, and Anna's parents hoped for a better life for their oldest child. She was sent to live with relatives who had left Hallig Hooge a few years before and were now doing quite well in the new country.

Lorenzen family.
Back l to r: Anna's parents
Christian and Johanna, Carl,
Louisa, Harold, Justina and Ed.

Anna's father, Christian, built her a simple, solid wooden box to serve as a trunk. It had a hinged cover and a tray on the left side to hold smaller items. A lock had been added for safekeeping, and Anna kept her key pinned to the inside lining of her dress. Across the front of the brownish-black stained box was written in an unusual, but beautifully crafted script:

Anna Sophia Lorenzen
c/o George Boysen
152 Main Street
Cambridgeport, Mass
North Amerika

Anna Sophia Lorenzen's Box

Anna lived with the Boysens and worked hard to do whatever she could to help her family who still struggled to survive in the old country. She faithfully sent boxes of goods that they could sell or trade for the practical things they needed to survive. Coffee was something she sent regularly, since it was very scarce in Germany at that time and was a valuable commodity. She saved all she could from her meager earnings, and as her savings grew she sent each of her brothers (one brother at a time) money for their passage to America. In a very few years she had brought Siegfried (Fred), Carl and Edward to the United States.

Anna Sophia Lorenzen and William Warren Doughty were married in Lynn, Mass., in 1878 and made their home at 211 Lynnfield Street in

Doughty's Corner General Store in Lynn, Massachusetts

Lynn. William was born in Bath, Maine, and his family owned a cottage at King's Point in West Bath. He moved from Bath to Lynn in the 1870s to look for work and found a job in a shoe shop there. He also found his dear little Anna who became his life companion and helpmate.

In time, Ma and Pa Doughty acquired several homes and property adjacent to theirs, and the corner on Lynnfield Street became known as, Doughty's Corner, as it is to this day. Anna, entrepreneur that she was, opened a store in the vacant building next to their home. The sign that ran along the top of the building read: Doughty's Corner General Store. The little store prospered and sold everything from Bond Bread to National Fireworks.

At King's Point in West Bath, Maine
Great-grandfather Philip A. Freeman holding Florence, Grandfather Philip G. Freeman, Great-grandparents: William & Anna S. (Lorenzen) Doughty. In back are Ruth, William & Philip Freeman

Like so many other couples William and Anna wanted children. After many years and several miscarriages they had two healthy daugh-

Phil & Flossie at Buena Vista

ters, Mythlene and Florence. The girls were known to friends and family as Mitty and Flossie, and Flossie became my grandmother.

Florence "Flossie" Doughty married Philip Gordon Freeman from Halifax, Nova Scotia, on September 11, 1911 in Lynn. They lived in Lynn and gave birth to three of their five children there.

William and Anna Doughty bought the saltwater farm in East Brunswick, Maine in 1917. My great-grandmother, Anna Sophia (Lorenzen) Doughty, fell in love with the saltwater farm at first sight. The farm reminded Anna of her family and their home at Lorenzwarft on the island of Hallig Hooge in northeastern Germany. William and Anna enjoyed long weekends and vacations at the farm they called "Buena Vista," and they looked forward to making it their permanent home when they retired.

A few years after William and Anna bought the farm in Maine their son-in-law, Philip, developed a problem with his lungs and wasn't well. Philip's doctor talked to the young couple about major improvements he'd seen in several of his patients who had moved away from the city to live near the ocean. Filled with hope and having faith in the doctor's advice my great-grandparents offered the farm at Woodward Point to my grandparents. In a very short time the Freemans packed up their family and moved from Lynn, Mass., to their new home in East Brunswick, Maine.

My father, Philip Albert Freeman, was the oldest son of Philip and Flossie. He was born June 11, 1913. The other children in the family were: Ruth, William, Florence and Janet. Florence was born at the farm on August 16, 1922. Five years later her sister, Janet, was born there on

Left: Nanny Flossie at Buena Vista feeding her turkeys.

Janet at the Farm

June 9, 1927. In December Janet developed a flu-like virus and died within the week. I was named for my father's baby sister who is buried with her father in the New Meadows Cemetery.

Brunswick Record June 14, 1923—New Meadows News

The spring term of school at Prince's Point closed today. Miss Clara Thomas, who has taught here for several terms, has proved a very efficient and successful teacher. Pupils not absent during the term are: Philip Freeman, Perley Alexander, Georgia Rush, Roland Rush, Walter Douglass, Walter Alexander, William Freeman and Emily Rush. Walter Douglas is the only scholar not absent a day for the year.

Brunswick Record June 21, 1923—New Meadows News

S. A. Lorenzen of Lynn, Mass., is visiting Mr. and Mrs. William W. Doughty.

Mrs. William W. Doughty returned home last week, after spending seven weeks at her home in Lynn, Mass.

Philip Freeman, New Meadows, and Osman J. Higgins, West Bath, are making extensive repairs at Camp Ashawaug; a girls' summer camp at Foster's Point, West Bath.

Ruth Freeman, secretary, and Scott Davis, health officer of the

Prince's Point School Health Club, attended the reception given the Kincaid School, winner of the country schools' award.

It was in the first days of January in 1932 that my grandfather, Philip Gordon Freeman, was taken to the Maine General Hospital in Portland, Maine. Eleven years had passed since he and his family had moved to Maine from Massachusetts. Philip was forty-four years old when he died of carcinoma of the lungs at the Maine General Hospital following a pre-surgical procedure.

Brunswick Record—January 7, 1932 – Philip Gordon Freeman

Philip Gordon Freeman of South Brunswick, died Monday night at the Maine General Hospital in Portland, following a surgical operation. Mr. Freeman, whose home was on the New Meadows River, had been in the insurance business for the past four years, being associated with the John Hancock Mutual Life Insurance Company and working from the Bath office. He had been in poor health for some time and because of this retired from the insurance business last August.

He was born in Cambridge, Mass., February 6, 1888, the son of Mr. and Mrs. Philip Albert Freeman. He attended Horton Academy in Wolfville, Nova Scotia and later studied Engineering at Dalhousie College in Halifax.

After returning to his native city he married Florence Doughty on September 11, 1911. For the past 11 years he had lived in Brunswick, engaging first in farming and later the insurance business. His work brought him in contact with a large number of people and he leaves many friends.

He is survived by his wife and parents, and four children, Ruth, Philip A., William and Florence, all of Brunswick; brothers, Percy of Cuyahoga Falls, Ohio, Harry, David and Herbert of Halifax; and five sisters, Mrs. Sophie Christopherson, Misses Kathleen and Elizabeth Freeman and Mrs. Clifford (Thora) Levy, all of Halifax and Mrs. Mildred West of Boston. Funeral services were held from the Universalist Church at 2:30 o'clock Thursday afternoon. Rev. Harold Merrill officiated. Burial was at the New Meadows Cemetery on the Gurnet Road.

Mrs. Anna Sophia Doughty Buried On Birthday

Lynn, Massachusetts

On her 82nd birthday, Mrs. Anna Sophia Lorenzen Doughty, widow of William Warren Doughty of 211 Lynnfield Street was buried yesterday afternoon in Pine Grove Cemetery.

Funeral Services for Mrs. Doughty, who died Sunday, October 3, 1937, were held at Lynnfield Street Baptist Church at 3:00 pm with Pastor Rev. Eaton P. Robertson officiating.

Solos "The Old Rugged Cross" and "In The Garden" were sung by Eugene Conley. The bearers included 6 nephews, Fred, Julius, Edward, William, Christian and George Lorenzen.

The casket was banked with flowers from neighbors, Lynnfield St. Baptist Church, Mr. and Mrs. Irving Clark and family, Mrs. John H. Clarke and daughter, Mr. and Mrs. Albert Harrington, Mr. and Mrs. Theodore Brackett, Fred Lorenzen and family, Mr. and Mrs. Frank Stowell, Mrs. Gaudette and family, Maple Lodge of Odd Ladies, Mr. and Mrs. John Bee, Mr. and Mrs. Julius Lorenzen, Mr. and Mrs. Everett Smith, Mr. and Mrs. William Freeman and family, Mr. and Mrs. Philip Freeman and family, Miss Nellie Connors, Miss Catherine Walsh, Mrs. Mildred West, Mrs. C. J. Lorenzen and George, Mr. and Mrs. Albert Boot, Mr. and Mrs. Edward Lorenzen and family, Helen McCauley, Gladys Parker, Louise Tufts, Barbara Phillips, Jacqueline Page, Marjorie Hamilton, Gertrude Mungund, Ruth Crosby, Mr. and Mrs. John Shoemaker, Mr. and Mrs. George Face, Mr. and Mrs. Charles Melanson, Mr. and Mrs. Ernest Towne, Mr. and Mrs. William Curtis, Mr. and Mrs. E. A. Tufts, C. J. Whitten, Mrs. Charles Butterworth and family, Mr. and Mrs. Melvin Coombs, Mr. and Mrs. Clarence Minott, C. W. Lorenzen, Mrs. Halliday and son, George Melanson, Mr. and Mrs. E. W. Park and daughter, Mildred, Mr. and Mrs Chester H. Young, Mr. and Mrs. Edward Lorenzen, Mr. and Mrs. Leo Barber, Mr. and Mrs. Louis Trull, Mr. and Mrs. Raymond Safford, Mr. and Mrs. John Davis and Mrs. Florence B. Freeman.

Mrs. Doughty is survived by a daughter, Mrs. Florence B. Freeman, 5 Grandchildren: Mrs. Everett Smith of Lynn, Mrs. Jessie Snow of

Saugus, Philip Freeman of Brunswick, Maine, William and Florence Freeman of Lynn; a brother, Edward L. of Cambridge and a sister, Caroline, in Germany.

Freeman Farm at Woodward Point in Brunswick, Maine
Pre-1857 Residence of G. Woodward

Approximate Date: Ell ca. 1790, Main House ca. 1830, Federal Massing, with Greek Revival entry

Maps: 1857 G Woodward, 1871 G Woodward, 1910 G T Woodward

1871 Directory: Gilbert Woodward, farmer, h. New Meadows Road

Reference Source: Pejepscot Historical Society – May 1987

Historic Preservation Survey – #39-44A

2
Our House at Bailey Island

I n the spring of 1939 Great-grandfather Elisha Leeman gave my mother a piece of his ten-acre plot on Bailey Island. His parents had divided thirty-two acres among three of their children: my great-grandfather Elisha, his sister Almira and brother George. The three siblings eventually married and had children. As their families grew the elders deeded enough land to each of their children to build a house.

As a result of this division of land our neighborhood was made up of Leemans and their offspring. At the top of the hill, up next to the main road, lived three sets

Phil, Selina, Gordon & Janet

of grandparents and great-grandparents. At the bottom of the hill were the homes of the descendants of Elisha, Almira and George Leeman.

Along with the gift of land in the spring of 1939 Grampy Leeman also loaned my mother $289 to buy the necessary materials to build a house. Grampy Leeman, Joe Pitts and my father built and framed the shell, and Uncle Ira White, a mason by trade, built a brick chimney that went up the center of the house. Our bathroom was a small outhouse.

Our Little House – 1944 – Toddler Connie

It was out the door and around to the back, and we referred to it as the "back-house." We moved into our house, as rough and unfinished as it was, in the fall of 1939.

It was a small cape-style house with white clapboards and a green shingled roof nestled amongst the white birch and spruce trees at the edge of the woods. The house was built on cedar posts and had no foundation or cellar. Each year before the weather turned really cold, we'd bank all around the house with fir and spruce boughs. This helped to insulate the floors and keep the cold out.

If you stood facing the front of our house, you would see two windows and a door. One of the windows was in the kitchen and the other in the living room. From the outside, on the far right side, were two steps to a small landing and the only entrance to our house. The door opened into the living room. Upon entering you would see a chair by the window on your left and a couch along the wall on the right. There was also a chair next to the couch in the corner between the back and side walls.

Centered on the wall above the couch hung the framed "Lindbergh Flight" print that always hung above our couch, no matter where we lived! I didn't know the significance of the picture until many years later.

Shortly after my parents were married my grandfather, **Philip** Gordon Freeman, gave the picture to my Dad to remind him of his dream to fly. It was an unfulfilled dream for my father **Philip**. But his son **Philip** got his private pilot's license, and our grandson **Philip** Achey did as well!

After my father's death I found the Lindbergh Flight print among my mother's things. I was taking apart a framed collage of historical family photos to have copies made and there, buried beneath the collage, was the Lindbergh Flight. It made a treasured gift for my brother, Philip Gordon, and it hangs on his wall to this day.

If you sat on our couch beneath the Lindbergh Flight picture you would face the center wall of the house. There were two doorways cut into the wall. . . one on the left and one on the

Kitchen view – Family friend Mike Doughty doing dishes.

right. Passing through the opening on the right, there was a short sideboard with open dish cupboards above. To the left of the sink, that was set into the sideboard, sat two 10-quart water pails. Usually a dipper was floating on the top of one of the pails. From the single-paned window over the sink you looked out on a path that went through the bushes and down to the backshore.

On the back wall across from the sideboard that held our two water pails was a set of stairs leading to our two small bedrooms up under the eaves. An old oak icebox was built into the center wall under the stairs directly across from the wood stove. There were two windows in the other end of the kitchen, and the back corner of the kitchen held the table and chairs where we ate all our meals.

The kitchen wood stove was our only source of heat, and it kept the small house comfortably warm. The top surface of the stove served as a cook top and was fairly easy to use. You could regulate the heat from Hi to Low by moving the cooking pot or kettle from the front to the back of the stove. Regulating the temperature of the oven was a bit more difficult. You couldn't just set a dial to the desired temperature and wait a few minutes for the oven to preheat. It took years of experience to learn which wood to use and how much was needed to get the right temperature and then to maintain that temperature while you were baking.

In order to cook supper for the family, make a pot of coffee or tea or simply to heat something up, meant lighting a fire in the wood stove. This wasn't a problem except during the hottest days of summer when a fire in the stove would heat up the whole house.

We lived in the house for quite a few years with no electricity. At the end of the day, when darkness set in, we'd light the Aladdin Lamp and smaller kerosene lamps for our light. The lamps had to be filled often; their wicks needed to be kept trimmed; and the smoke on the glass chimneys washed off to get the best light.

Being without electricity involved much more than not having electric lights! All the things we take for granted today were not available without electricity. There was no refrigerator, washing machine, dryer, iron, mixer or TV in our home. We did have a battery-powered radio that provided us with a bit of entertainment and gave us a glimpse of the world beyond our small Island.

After the death of our Grandfather Freeman in 1932, Nanny Flossie left the farm on Woodward Point Road in Brunswick and moved back to Lynn, Mass. In the late 1940s she married William Parker who had worked for Lynn Light and Power for many years. On one of their frequent visits to Maine, Bill Parker brought all the materials and the skills of his trade to wire our house. We truly were blessed with generous and skilled tradesmen in our family!

Thanks to our mother, our humble little house was always a real home. The sun sparkled and shone through clean kitchen windows where homemade yellow and white gingham curtains hung. A long gathered skirt made of the same material hung along the linoleum covered counter down to the floor. Since there were no cupboard doors, the curtain hid the unsightly sink drain, its trap and the well-used pots and pans below. The living room and kitchen floors were both covered with the same maroon colored linoleum that took a good shine when freshly washed and waxed.

In the back corner of the kitchen there was a white drop-leaf table that could seat our family of six. Every few years, in the spring, Mum would get out a can of white enamel paint and freshen up the woodwork and the table and chairs. She'd finish the job with colorful little decals of fruits and vegetables for the backs of the chairs.

We had a nice lawn at home, and Mum always kept flowers planted in the rock garden and window boxes that Dad had made for her. She liked to plant "hens and chickens" in the

Mum working in her garden.

crevices of the exposed ledges under the trees in front of the house. Her perennial garden circled our largest birch tree, and its perimeter was framed with special rocks brought home from the backshore.

First thing in the spring Mum was able to add a bit of variety to her perennial garden. She'd walk down to Cedar Island to pick "pig-weed" greens for supper above the ledges there. If she had time she'd stop on her way home and thin out a few flower gardens at the empty summer cottages. She always managed to leave enough room in her bag of greens for a few new perennials.

We kept our perishable foods in the wooden icebox in the kitchen. During the summer months an iceman would come to the Island from Brunswick to deliver ice right to our door. The block ice lasted much longer than the ice we used in the winter months, which was cut from the frozen pond at Grampy Leeman's pit next door.

Sometimes I'd go with my father and brother Gordon when they went to get ice from the pit. I liked watching them chop away at the ice with a long-handled axe. It was hard work getting the big chunks of ice, but the bigger the pieces the longer it lasted. When the pail was full they'd carry it home and dump it into the pan in the bottom of the icebox.

For a real treat on a Sunday afternoon we'd use the ice from the pit to make ice cream. While we were getting ice our mother would mix all the ingredients and pour them into the metal container inside the wooden bucket. When we got back from the pit they'd pack the ice all around the container and sprinkle it with rock salt. Then it was up to us! Each of us kids took turns cranking the handle that turned the paddles inside the ice-cream container. We knew when it got really hard to turn the handle that it wouldn't be long before we'd be sitting at the table with a nice big bowl of Grape-Nut ice cream.

3
World War II Years

In March of 1943 during World War II my father went to work in the Portland shipyard as part of the war effort. We moved from our little house on Bailey Island into a trailer park for shipyard employees in Cape Elizabeth, Maine.

There was a school in the trailer park, and even though I didn't turn five until December of that year they let me attend school there. The following year when we came back to the Island I was able to go right into the first grade. Due to starting school early I was always the youngest one in the class, right on through high school.

My sister Connie was born on May 7, 1943 at Maine General Hospital in Portland. The first summer of her life she got very sick with infectious diarrhea and had to be hospitalized. The doctors did all they could for her, but she continued to get worse and almost died. Things were critical when the young doctor on duty for the weekend called my parents in for a consultation. He needed and received their permission to try something totally new as "a last resort." The doctor injected massive doses of vitamins directly into her spine, and miraculously, the treatment worked! She got better and finally was well enough to come home.

When we moved back to the house on Bailey Island in the fall of 1944 my brother Gordon was ten; I was almost six; and Connie was one year and four months. Mum was six months pregnant.

On December 10, 1944 my little brother Wayne Alan Freeman was

WWII Victory celebration at the Orr's and Bailey Island Bridge

born at the old Brunswick Hospital on the corner of Union and Cumberland Streets. A month later my father left the house one morning and didn't come back. With no income and four children to care for and support, Mum had no choice but to find a job.

Dad's brother Bill spoke to her about a job opening at a supermarket near their home in Bath. They told her if she got the job she could stay with them, and Aunt Shirley would take care of Connie and Wayne while she worked. Mum applied for the cashier position and was hired.

Since Gordon and I attended school on Bailey Island, we stayed up across the field with Nanny Shea and Grampy Leeman. On weekends Mum would pack up Connie and Wayne and come back to our house on the Island so we could all be together as a family for a few days.

After my father had been away from home for several months, my mother heard rumors that he had joined the navy. In time she received a letter from his commanding officer verifying the rumors. She now had Dad's address and knew that he was in basic training in the U.S. Navy.

In June of 1945, six months after he had left his family, my father came home. I was outside playing when I first saw him. He was up past the well in the field, at the top of the hill. I just stood there in the play-

Above: Dad in Uniform with Mum. Below: Me in the Playhouse

house and watched as he made his way down across the field and through the path by the Perry's house. I didn't dare to get excited or think of running in the house to tell my mother or even to run and meet him! Since he'd been gone I'd dreamed of him coming home, just like this, only to wake up and find it wasn't true.

He saw me in the playhouse about the same time I knew for sure it was really him. I cried out, "Daddy, you're home!" Hesitantly, he picked up his step, and as he did his arms opened wide. I ran to him, and he scooped me up into his strong arms and held me close. He smelled so good!

"Daddy, I waited a long time for you to come home. Where did you go? Were you lost? I missed you so much. Oh, I love you, Daddy! And I don't suck my thumb anymore and my two front teeth came out and the tooth fairy came and gave me two quarters under my pillow and

I've tried to be a real good girl and help Mum with the babies, and, and…" His cheeks were wet against my silky blonde hair. "Oh, Janet. Oh, my little princess. Daddy has missed you so much! How did you get so big so fast? Let me look at you. Really, no front teeth and you don't suck your thumb anymore! I'm so proud of you!"

Reluctantly, he put me down, and with my small hand in his we walked through the path up to the house together. My mother must have loved my father very much because she forgave him and took him back into her life and ours. We were all so happy to have him back home, and it felt so good to be a family again.

Years later Mum said, "I don't know if I did the right thing or not, but he looked so good to me and life had been so hard and lonely with him gone! He was sober and looked fresh and healthy from boot camp and so very handsome in his navy uniform. While the two of you stood there waiting in the doorway, with you holding onto him for dear life, I made my decision. The war was raging in Europe, and I knew he'd only have a short time home before his leave was up and he'd be shipped overseas. What else could I have done?"

4
Health and Dental Care

Before I could go to the Bailey Island School I had to have an inoculation and a vaccination. Dr. Webb and Miss Higgins were in charge of the free clinic that was held each year at the school on Bailey Island. My mother and the doctor decided to place the vaccination on my upper thigh, which was done quite often at that time. It didn't work out so well for me since I developed a long-lasting infection and was left with a good-sized scar.

When I went to Dr. Webb for my preschool shots it was only the second time I'd been seen by a doctor since birth. The first time was when I fell from a highchair and broke my collarbone. I was 18 months old. I went through all of the childhood diseases (old-fashioned measles, whooping cough, chicken pox and German measles) without being seen by a doctor. It wasn't until 1957 when I was 18 years old and preparing to get married that I had my first doctor's office experience. At that time it was compulsory to have a blood test before getting married in the state of Maine.

Dental clinics for the Bailey Island children were also held during the summer months. Dr. Parker Luckey was a dentist who had a practice and winter home in Paterson, New Jersey. He set up an office with a dentist chair and all the necessary equipment in a small building behind his summer home on the Island.

Dr. Luckey's nephew, Pete Smith, was also a dentist and practiced

Dental Clinic

Doreen C
Denise Beaulieu
Alice H
Nancy
Pat Shea
Donna
Jeff Johnson
Steve
Sandra S
Joyce Murray
Karen
1948

Annual Free
Dental Clinic

dentistry out of state. Every summer he would hold a free clinic in his uncle's office for the Island children. He volunteered his services and time while on vacation with his family at their summer cottage. Parents of Island children waited until summer each year to have their children's teeth checked and attended to by Dr. Smith.

As a kid, my front teeth were separated and stuck out a bit. When I got old enough to be concerned and had been called "Bucky" a few times, I thought maybe the braces some of the summer kids had on their teeth would help.

Over the summer months I saved enough money to pay for an appointment with the dentist on Orr's Island. He checked my teeth and sent me home with a few packages of small rubber bands and instructions on how to use them. That was about the closest I ever got to a professional opinion or braces on my teeth!

5
Bailey Island School

I spent most of my elementary school years at the Bailey Island School. I walked to and from school, but my brother Gordon was old enough to take his bike. I always remember him racing up the hill on his bike and me chasing after him and yelling for him to "wait up!"

When I went to the Bailey Island School there were two floors with one large classroom on each floor. Vara Leeman taught the four to five lower grades downstairs, and Margaret Skillings taught the upper grades on the second floor.

The school had two outside doors. The one on the left was used for the upstairs kids, and the smaller kids came in on the right. As we came in through the door there was a hall in the entryway where we hung our jackets and coats on one of the black hooks they'd mounted on the wall about four feet from the floor. On rainy days or during the winter months we wore boots that went over our shoes. They were usually black or brown and we called them overshoes. Some were pulled on and others had buckles that opened in the front. We had to take off our boots before going into the classroom and put them up against the wall beneath our coats.

I can still picture our big classroom. It took up all of the downstairs of the Bailey Island School. Mrs. Leeman's big desk stood in the very front of the room, and off to the side were the water cooler and the

1930 – 31 Grammar Room at Bailey Island. Front to Back: Franklin Lord, Elroy F. Doughty, John L. Murray, Paul Skillings, Jim Shea, Georgie Smith, Ernestine Lubee, Dorothea Skillings, Lila Baker, Jeanette Johnson, Geraldine R. Johnson, Raymond Johnson, Teacher: Margaret Black Skillings, Dorothy Doughty, Mabel Clary, Selina Shea

Vara Leeman's Classroom – 1944
Front to Back: Sandra Stevens, Sally Murray, Nancy Johnson, Jerry Leeman, Donna Leeman, Janet Freeman, Corrine Johnson, Joseph Orr, Gordon Freeman, Ruth V. Johnson, Donald Rogers & Teacher: Vara Leeman

rusty cast iron woodstove. The stove was taller than most stoves today and had a rounded belly with a door that opened in the front like a big mouth through which you'd feed the wood. I was always fascinated by the long metal stovepipe that led from the back of the stove up to the high ceiling above. Wires held the stovepipe secure as it traveled along the ceiling from the front of the room to the back where the pipe would eventually find its way into the chimney.

There was no plumbing in the school, and although the bathrooms were indoors, they were outhouses. There was one for the boys and one for the girls. Each bathroom had two or three holes which made it possible for more than one child to go at the same time! When we needed

c. Vara Leeman's 3rd, 4th & 5th Grades − 1946-47
Front to Back: William Dunlap, Edwin Dunlap, Oliver O'Neil, Wayne Johnson, Don Rogers, Jerry Leeman, Richard Crowe, Joseph Orr, Nancy Johnson, Sandra Williams, Sandra Stevens, Patricia Taylor, Janet Freeman, Judy Harris, Shirley Shea, Donna Leeman, Yvonne Sylvester, Bucky Swan, Russell Wilson, Alfred Perry, Evelyn Moody, Doreen Cotter, Mary Crowley, Alice Herrick, Lucille Snow, Ruth Johnson, Bob Stevens, Carol Thurston, Pat Shea, Ruth V. Johnson, Glennis Reid, Madelyn Stilphen & Lorraine Snow

to be excused during class to go to the bathroom, we were told to raise our hand and hold up one finger if we had to "P" and two fingers if we had to do something else. I always wondered about the upstairs bathrooms. They must have been built to extend beyond the outside wall of the building (kind of like a laundry chute) for everything to make its way down below to the holding box!

Vara Leeman was my teacher from the first grade through the fourth. She was married to my grandmother's cousin, Alton Leeman, and they lived very close to the school in a neat little white cape-style house with green shutters. Mrs. Leeman was a good-sized woman in height as well as girth. She had neatly trimmed medium black hair that took a good permanent wave and always looked the same. She wore wire-rimmed glasses and neat dark-colored dresses and blouses with large lace edged collars that outlined her open neckline. She always tucked her tatted

Bailey Island School – Lower Grades – 1949
Front to Back: Jim Doughty, Willis Painton, Larry Johnson, John ("Teddy") Bear, David
Skillings, Bill Coombs, Ira Leeman, Wayne Dudley, Steve Johnson, Jackie Williams, Sue
Oliver, Martha Drake, Lauretta Brown, Pearl Stilphen, Joyce Murray, Donna Dudley,
Diane Johnson, Janice Wilson, Joyce Rose Doughty, Joyce Stilphen, Irene Richardson,
Ann Doughty, Paulette Dudley, Patty Catlin, Phyllis Johnson, Polly Leeman, Jane Oliver,
Blanche Stilphen, Connie Freeman, Sandra Jones, Sharon Johnson, Norma Huff, Chip
Black, Joe Harris, Tommy Richards, Bob Johnson, Neil Durant, Stanley Hargraves,
Ernest Hilman, Pete Rogers & Sonny Bailey

edged hankies inside the front of her blouse or underneath the belt of her dress or skirt. She wore practical black leather shoes with a good sturdy heel that laced up the center. They must have been fashionable at that time because my Nanny Shea wore the same style shoe.

Our school day would begin with the Lord's Prayer right after attendance had been taken. Then Mrs. Leeman would read aloud one of the psalms from her Bible. At the end of the psalm we'd all stand up and face the flag in the corner of the room. We'd recite the Pledge of Allegiance with our right hand held up to our forehead and our thumb tucked under our fingers.

Mrs. Leeman also checked us each day to see if our hair had been combed and our hands, ears, necks and fingernails were clean. Periodic checks for head-lice were made if a problem had been reported, and quite often there were problems.

We had several chores at school and were responsible for that job all week. One of the assigned jobs was to take care of the flag each day. First thing in the morning you'd get the flag from the closet and bring it outside to hoist it up to the top of the flagpole in the schoolyard. Two students were always assigned to flag detail. One of the first things we were taught about our country's flag was to treat it with respect. We also learned the correct way to fold the flag and to be very careful not to let it touch the ground. If you were in charge of the flag for the week, it was up to you to bring the flag in at the end of the day or to run outside and bring it in earlier if it looked like bad weather was threatening.

Keeping the blackboards erased and stocked with chalk and clean erasers was another one of our assigned chores for the week. Black slate chalkboards covered the front walls of the classroom. When I was erasing the boards it never failed that one of my fingers would slip away from the eraser and a fingernail would screech down across the blackboard. It always gave me "goose bumps" and got a reaction from the kids and Mrs. Leeman. After erasing all the blackboards, we'd take the erasers outside to clean them of their dust. First we'd bang them together and then against the side of the white school building. White puffy clouds of chalk dust filled the air around us.

I especially remember looking forward to our Friday afternoon art classes and spelling bees. I loved the spelling bees because I did pretty well. We'd all stand up along one side of the room. Whenever someone misspelled a word, he or she had to sit down. It felt good, and I was proud when I got to be one of the last kids standing there.

Our art classes were usually spent working on something for the upcoming holiday. Most of our projects were made with construction paper, match boxes, crepe paper and crayons. We made valentines, May baskets, Easter eggs and jack-o-lanterns.

On Valentine's Day Mrs. Leeman's desk would hold a big cardboard box that we'd covered earlier with red and white crepe paper and decorated with our homemade valentines. On the "big day" we'd bring our valentines from home and drop them through the slot in the top of the box for our teacher and all of our friends. It was fun, but it was also a bit of a popularity contest. The kids who got a lot of valentines were happy, but those who got just a few, or none at all, were left feeling a little sad and left out.

Halloween at school was always fun. We'd have a party in our classroom on the Friday before Halloween and got to play all kinds of games. One of our favorites was bobbing for apples. Early on the morning of our party Mrs. Leeman's husband Alton would bring in a large galvanized washtub and a box of apples that he'd set on the floor next to Mrs. Leeman's desk. Just before the party was to begin, Mrs. Leeman would send a couple of the bigger boys to carry a few buckets of water from the well next door to fill the washtub.

We had a lot of fun bobbing for apples, but certain rules had to be followed. First of all we had to get in a line and keep our hands clasped behind our backs. When it was finally our turn, we'd try to get an apple out of the water with just our teeth. The trick was to find an apple with a long stem, bite on it and lift it out. It sounds easy, but it's not! In trying to grab the stem, the apple would usually sink below the surface of the water and your face would go down with it. Determined "apple bobbers" always went under, and the more times we dunked the more the kids laughed. And, if Mrs. Leeman turned her back for a minute, one of the boys would jump at the chance to give someone's head a quick little dunk down into the water. When Mrs. Leeman looked to see who the culprit was, he looked very innocent talking with the kid behind him.

If we had clothesline, all we needed for another game we played was string and doughnuts. We would string the clothesline across the room and then tie varying lengths of string at different intervals so that they would hang down from the clothesline. Doughnuts were then tied to the strings. With our hands behind our backs, we would try to get a doughnut that was at the right height for us to grab with our teeth. If I remember correctly, the object of the game was to see who could eat the doughnut off the string first.

BEFORE — The old school house on Bailey Island, which holds many memories for local residents, looked like this in June 1965, just before local builder-lobsterman George Stevens started an extensive remodeling project to convert it into a private home, with ground floor apartment space. (Fides photo)

AFTER — Today, the old schoolhouse stands above Mackerel Cove with a clean new face. The Stevens' recently moved into the second floor of the former school which was originally built in the 1890's. (Hinckley photo)

Picture of the Bailey Island School as it appeared in the Times Record (date unknown).

Nancy Johnson and I were best friends from our very first days at the Bailey Island School. By the time we were in the fourth grade Mrs. Leeman hired us to do janitorial work for her. At the end of each school day we'd sweep our big classroom, dust around the desks and wash down the blackboards.

Mrs. Leeman told us we should always sweep first because it gave the dust a chance to settle. We each had our own broom, and with Nancy on one side of the room and me on the other we made a game of how fast we could finish our side and meet in the middle. It took us quite awhile to sweep the big room and to do it right! Although we were young and small, we tried to do a good job and follow Mrs. Leeman's instructions.

We'd get our reward every Friday afternoon for our week's work. Mrs. Leeman always had a shiny new quarter for each of us. Out the door running, we'd get to the store as fast as we could to buy a small brown paper bag full of penny candy. We just knew, if we didn't hurry, that quarter would "burn a hole" in our pockets!

6

Growing Up on Bailey Island

Ercil, Me & Gordon in the Playhouse

When we were little kids it seems like we always had a playhouse. There was an area just off the south edge of our lawn that we called our playhouse. It wasn't a real playhouse by today's definition, but a place where we played for hours at a time when we were little. Over time Dad filled our sandbox with white sand he'd carried in buckets up the path from the beach at Cedar Island.

Mum always seemed to find just the right toys for the playhouse when she spring-cleaned the kitchen. A collection of empty spice tins, an old salt shaker, worn out soup and serving spoons, dented and mended pots and pans that still leaked, cups with no handles, and old pie tins and canisters made us happy. As we got older we pretended the cleared areas in the junipers and bayberry bushes were the rooms of our house, and this added another dimension to our world of pretend.

I enjoyed my first taste of freedom as a little girl when I was allowed to visit the homes of our neighborhood. The older folks would ask me

Connie & Wayne – Lunch in the Nook

to recite a poem or sing a little song for them. I would usually sing, "I'm a Little Teapot," and act it out for them. I liked all the attention, and I'd usually get a cookie for my command performance. At one point my mother threatened to make me wear a little sign that said, "Please do not feed Janet." I was already short, but like my little song, I was getting "short and stout."

As we got older we were able to venture out a bit more on our own and play with the kids in the neighborhood. Most of the kids we played with and grew up with were our third and fourth cousins. We all went to the same school, church and Sunday School classes.

In the spring, with the smell of burnt grass all around us, we played games of baseball and tag out in the field. We played hopscotch, marbles, jacks and jump rope at Jessie and Herb's or in Elsie and Arn's driveway. When hopscotch season came around we'd try to find a nice flat, smooth stone to use for our "pitch." With the right piece we could pitch more accurately into the hopscotch squares. The "pitch" could not land on the lines or outside the squares that had been drawn so carefully in the dirt driveway with a wooden stick.

Jessie and Herb Leeman had three kids. June was the oldest, Polly was next, and Ira was the youngest. Their family had a henhouse where they kept hens for eggs until one spring they decided the hens were no longer worth the trouble. The Leeman girls and I got the bright idea of turning the empty henhouse into a playhouse! After we got permission from Jessie and Herb, we went to work.

We scraped, swept, scrubbed and washed the tiny windows. All the ladies in the neighborhood gave us their discarded cracked dishes, cups, pans, empty extract bottles, spice tins, salt, pepper and oatmeal boxes. Nanny Shea even gave us some scraps of bright cotton calico from her ragbag that we tacked up to the clean windows for curtains. We loved our little playhouse. But, no matter how much we cleaned and pretended not to notice, it always smelled like a henhouse!

Monday was wash-day in our neighborhood. With some of the ladies it was sort of a status symbol to see who could get their wash hung out on the clothesline before anyone else. Some said that Jessie Leeman probably did hers the night before just to be first!

Throughout the day, when the ladies walked to the post office or the store, they'd have short visits with each other along the way. The main topic of conversation for the day was usually Monday's wash. "I got my clothes in early today and, got it all folded and put away," one would say. Her neighbor might answer, "I got my sheets in off the line, the beds all made up nice 'n fresh and my basket of ironing is sitting there all ready for me to get to first thing in the morning." A likely response to this would be, "I like to get my ironing done right after it comes in off the line." An easy supper of Saturday night's leftover baked beans was the usual fare for Monday nights after a day of laundry.

My mother didn't have the luxury of a washing machine at home. Our dirty laundry had to be carried up across the field to Grampy Leeman's house. Nanny's wringer washing machine and galvanized washtubs for rinsing would be set up in the middle of the kitchen floor on washday. It was a real luxury to have a hand-pump at the sink that pumped water up from the cistern in the cellar instead of having to carry the water from the well in the field. After the clothes were washed,

Me Picking Blueberries

rinsed and put through the wringer for the last time, Mum would bring the wet clothes home to hang on our clotheslines between the birch trees.

Most of the kids in our neighborhood took swimming lessons at Cedar Beach in the summer and played in the snow together in the winter. After a good snowstorm we'd go sliding or skiing on Aunt Mamie's hill or down across the field. Sometimes we'd slide down Robin Hood Road across from the Log Cabin Lodge. It was a dirt road then leading to Water Cove, Robin Hood Inn and the beach at Cedar Island. (I still want to call it Dr. McCarty's Road, even though it hasn't been called that for years.)

In the early years a map showing our little section of the Island would have included the following landmarks: the well, the apple tree, Uncle Jim Perry's barn, the field, Grampy's garden and the gravel pit. There were also the homes of Jessie and Herb, Elsie and Arn, Madeline and Boog, Aunt Mamie, and Jim Thomas.

Other places of significance were the Bailey Island Cemetery, Dr. McCarty's Road, the spring, Robin Hood Inn, Water Cove, Grampy Leeman's Fishhouse, Cedar Island, Little Cedar, Oceanside or the Backshore. These familiar landmarks were the highlights of our immediate surroundings when we were small.

In the late summer we liked to go blueberrying on the hill across the road from Grampy Leeman's house. The area we called Blueberry Hill was on the western side of Route 24 between the Log Cabin Lodge and the Bailey Island Cemetery. When the blueberries were plentiful we could pick as many as we wanted there for most of the season. We brought home

Uncle Jim Perry Clearing a Field

some for our mothers to use for baking but sold most of what we picked to the summer people and the local restaurants for fifty cents a quart. The restaurants usually took all we could pick and were happy to get them for their blueberry buckles, cobblers, muffins and pies.

We'd climb the tree up in the middle of Uncle Jim Perry's field and help ourselves to as many apples as we wanted. The apples were small and wormy, but we ate them just the same. If we got a chance we sometimes snitched strips of dried fish from his drying racks that were set up between his house and the barn where he always kept a heifer and a couple of cows for milk.

The Perry's house was a fun place to visit, and it smelled a lot like the cats that lived there. Uncle Jim Perry loved his cats. No matter where you'd look, you'd see a cat! They were perched on top of the refrigerator, asleep on the counters, tables and chairs, and under the tables and chairs. They were in the corners and on the big homemade braided rug in the middle of the kitchen floor.

Uncle Jim had his own way of talking to his cats, and he was always communicating with them. When he talked to them, it sounded something like, "oom, oom, unh, unh, unh, oom." We loved going there to be entertained by all the cats and Uncle Jim's unusual cat lingo. Trying to be polite, we'd hold back our giggles until we were safely outside.

Aunt Mamie's House - 1763

After supper we'd run up across the field to the barn hoping to get there before Uncle Jim finished milking the cows. It was fun to watch him milk, and when he was finished he'd fill the sauce dishes on the barn floor from his pail of warm milk. The barn cats and their little ones purred contentedly and Uncle Jim continued talking to them softly as they licked the saucers clean.

My great aunt, Mamie Leeman, lived in one of the oldest houses (if not the oldest) on Bailey Island. It was built in 1763, and up in the peak of the house facing the main road it had a small sign that said so. Aunt Mamie was the widow of Grampy Leeman's brother George who had died some years before. As children we were fascinated with Aunt Mamie because she was such a lady. She always wore pretty dresses and was a beautiful older woman. She had snow-white hair that she swept up into a French twist in the back and her eyes were as blue as the waters of Casco Bay.

Whenever we came to visit she always acted so happy to see us there at her door. She'd welcome us into her home and insist that we come in and stay for awhile as she'd whisk our jackets away to hang them on the hooks by the door. In no time at all she'd have a batch of fudge cooking on the top of the stove, stirring it every few minutes till it got to just the right temperature. Then she'd add a big dollop of butter or peanut butter and set it aside to cool. While we were waiting for the much-anticipated fudge to be ready, she'd offer to play the piano for us. At first she'd sing alone in her high, scratchy voice. But after awhile she encouraged us to sing along with her, and we'd forget our shyness and join in. It was always such a merry, happy time.

Aunt Mamie always knew, without even looking, when the fudge had cooled enough. She'd get up from the piano stool and go out into the kitchen for one last stir before she poured it into the pan she had prepared earlier. After the fudge had set for awhile she'd cut each of us a big piece. It was the best fudge ever! Her blue eyes sparkled when she teased us about the one secret ingredient she always added to her fudge that made it so special. She gave each of us a copy of her recipe but never did tell us what the secret ingredient was. I think, without a doubt, it was love.

In the winter months, we'd go ice skating in the gravel pit as soon as the ice was tested and declared safe by one of the parents. On school days we'd skate right after school but had to stay in after supper to do a little homework and go to bed early. We loved the freedom of the weekends when we could skate after dark. The older kids would make a huge bonfire on the ice using whatever wood they could scrounge up in the neighborhood, and when the wood got scarce one of the boys would round up an old tire or two to throw on the fire.

We'd warm our hands and feet by the fire, and the flames would light up the whole pond. The black sludge and soot from the burning tires would fill the night air and cover the ice of the pond and everything nearby with a black film. At the end of the fun-filled night of exercise and play we'd head for home, wondering if our weakened ankles and tired legs would get us there. The once colorful hand-knit woolen mittens that we wore and the knees and seats of our pants were black with soot. Our big eyes looked out from blackened faces that resembled the family of raccoons we'd seen in the compost pile last summer.

Grampy Leeman's pit was once a working pit and a good source of gravel. My father was 21 and working in the gravel pit in the spring of 1934 when my brother Philip Gordon was born. His job was to load gravel onto trucks with a hand shovel. The gravel was used for driveways and as a base for the road they were building on the Island.

I don't remember the pit when it was used as a source of gravel. I only remember it as a big hole in the ground that had two-thirds of its banks covered with discarded appliances, motors, cars, household trash and garbage. For those of us in the neighborhood, it was our dump. The families at the top of the hill would dump their garbage and anything else they wanted to get rid of over the side of the upper part, while we at the bottom of the field would dump our refuse over the lower banks. Because of the garbage that was dumped there regularly, it attracted a lot of rats. A favorite pastime of one of the families of third and fourth cousins in the neighborhood was to spend the afternoon at the gravel pit shooting rats! Not a pleasant thought, but it did keep the rat population down.

Bailey Island was a pretty special place to be a child in the 1940s. We knew or were related to just about everyone on Bailey Island and "No Trespassing" signs were nonexistent. At a very young age we were free to safely roam the Island from one end to the other.

As we grew our map of familiar places also grew. It now included the Union Church, Bailey Island School, Library Hall, Uncle Harold and Aunt Jo's, Joe Lubee's, Perley Sinnett's, the Steamboat Wharf, Sinnett's Store and Post Office, Ocean View and Driftwood Hotels, and the Yale Shoppe.

On our walks to the Post Office or the store we felt free to stop at almost any house along the way to use someone's bathroom, get a drink of water or warm our hands next to a warm stove. We were usually welcomed warmly.

I remember one cold winter day especially well. I was on my way to Joe Lubee's store and had cut across the field by Aunt Mamie and Wash Doughty's. After following the path up the hill in back of Rip and Emma Black's house, I went around to the front door and knocked. Emma came to the door right away and looked happy to see me there. She said, "Janet, what a nice surprise! Please take off your coat and stay for a bit. I just now took a sheet of raisin cookies out of the oven, and I'm going to have a cup of tea and make you a nice cup of hot chocolate. We'll get you warmed up and then you can be on your way." Needless to say, Emma and Rip Black's house was one of my favorite stops.

Most Islanders would gather in the morning at Sinnett's Store and Post Office down at the old steamboat wharf on the eastern side of Mackerel Cove. Folks usually got there early enough to watch the steamboat come into the cove and make its approach to the wharf. Once the

Steamboat Wharf at Mackerel Cove.

boat was in and tied up to the pilings on the wharf, the gangplank would be lowered into place. Those on shore were most interested to see who was getting off the boat. After the passengers had disembarked the locals stood around and visited their neighbors and friends while the steamboat crew unloaded the cargo from Portland.

Mr. Sinnett or one of his helpers waited in Sinnett's truck on the wharf to haul the heavy mailbags and cases of groceries and produce up to the store and Post Office. After the steamboat was unloaded of its passengers and cargo everyone would head up to the store and Post Office to wait for the mail to be sorted. As Mr. Sinnett deposited the pieces of mail in the small numbered boxes, anxious folks stood by talking and catching up with the Island news and gossip while they watched their box for a long-awaited letter or a dreaded bill.

When the day's sorting was done Mr. Sinnett would raise the closed, roll-top window with a clatter. Everyone knew he was now available to sell stamps, weigh packages, and get mail and packages for those needing assistance. After everyone had their mail and picked up a few things from the store, they'd get ready to walk up the steep steamboat wharf hill and head for home. With their final goodbyes and "see you tomorrow's," they left each other feeling content and secure in their connection with the Island and its people.

Brunswick Record - Bailey Island News – March 23, 1950

E.E. Sinnett's Store at the wharf is all set for spring. An 8-foot deep freeze was delivered on Monday and is now stocked with fresh frozen meats, seafood, fruits, vegetables and ice cream. To add a further spring-like touch, flower, grass and vegetable seeds are on display.

Years later my friend Nancy Johnson Jensen and I paid Clayton Johnson a short visit one afternoon on March 3, 2001. We were talking about the old Steamboat Wharf at Mackerel Cove and Clayt shared the following story with us:

"Well, it kinda' goes like this... Winona ("Non") and I hadn't been married very long, and I must have been just about 20, when I was working for Sinnett down at the Steamboat Wharf. He had me drivin' a truck for the store and the wharf. This day I'd gone for a load of ice. I drove down onto the wharf and right up to the shed where the ice was stored. I got it all unloaded and saw-dusted down good and hopped back into the truck.

"Well, I went to turn that truck around and I braked and clutched. Then I let up on the clutch and let me tell you, when those tires hit that patch of oil on the wharf, that truck, with me at the wheel, slid right off the end of the wharf.

"On the way down I had presence of mind enough to figure I'd better get out fast. I did just that and jumped out! Let me tell you, it took a few men, a chain-fall and some time before we got that truck up out of the water and back onto the wharf!"

7
Canning Season

Mum's blond hair was damp, and she looked hot and tired standing there in her apron-covered, faded housedress. The heat coming from the fire in the woodstove and the canning kettle of boiling water filled the kitchen with steam. I remember coming in from outside to watch my parents prepare the fish for canning. While I sat on the stairs in the kitchen close to my mother and the sink, I drew pictures and wrote my name on the fogged up window next to me.

I didn't like the smells of the blood and guts from the mackerel Dad had been cleaning in the kitchen. Piles of tails, entrails and mackerel heads with staring eyes looked out from the bloody sink. The cleaned mackerel soaked in the gray enamel dishpan full of clear cold water waiting to go into the prepared salty brine for awhile. Then they would be taken out and plunged into boiling water for several minutes. Packing the mackerel into hot, sterile one-quart canning jars was the final step before processing and preserving the mackerel in the pressure cooker.

Canning mackerel was only one of the many foods my mother preserved for winter. Almost all of the canning and preserving was done during the hot summer months using a woodstove and carrying water down to our house from the well up in the middle of the field.

Our shelves under the stairs held a wide variety of foods put away for the winter. I remember big jars of tuna cut up into chunks, breasts of wild ducks and seabirds, dandelion greens and different kinds of pickles, applesauce, and jams and jellies made from blueberries, raspberries and blackberries.

In the fall during hunting season someone in the family would usually get a deer. Using the meat from the neck of a deer, along with apples, raisins, spices and suet, Mum would make "Uncle Harold's Mince Meat."

There was always an abundance of fish, clams, mussels and seabirds. In the summer wild blueberries, raspberries and blackberries were plentiful, and we felt free to pick anywhere on the Island. Old folks and families going through hard times never went hungry or did without, no matter how poor or needy they might find themselves.

A neighbor, friend or relative would always come by with a bucket, bowl or bag of mackerel, berries, vegetables, or whatever else might be in season at the time. The sharing of whatever was plentiful was just a way of life for the people of the Island.

Brunswick Record – July 26, 1945
Tuna Fish Is Popular Dish During The Meat Shortage

Many who thought fresh tuna unfit for human consumption are discovering they actually like it. Local ladies believe tuna, which is bloody and oily, is best if soaked in salt water for about four hours and then washed off in fresh water prior to cooking. After this process the fish is ready to be broiled, baked and stuffed or cooked in any number of ways.

Over 100 of the big fish were caught on one day last week between Small Point and Bailey Island. Star fishermen for the season up to the middle of this week are Oscar Gilliam and son, Merle of Phippsburg, with Jesse Johnson, Albert Smith, Carl Smith and Clayton Johnson of Bailey Island close runners-up. Last Saturday the Gilliams landed 12 tuna-fish. The season's average tuna weighs 500 pounds and most commercial fishermen report one to four caught daily.

Mackerel, salmon and sardine fishing are excellent this year, while lobstering, clamming and the sea moss industries are proving alluring to many Mainers. A number of men have quit regular jobs for the more exciting and lucrative field fishing is providing. One Brunswick boy reported a net return of $240 at the end of a recent week of lobstering.

8
Well in the Field

There was absolutely no plumbing in our house. By this I mean we had no bathroom and there were no faucets at the long white cast iron sink in the kitchen. All of our water was brought into the house in two ten-quart galvanized buckets that had to be filled and carried down to our house from the well that was located up in the middle of the field. This well was about 600 to 700 feet from our house and was used by most of the people in the neighborhood. It was a hand-dug well, faced with rocks, about 25 feet deep.

There was a weathered gray wooden house built around the well with a hinged cover. When the cover was lifted there was a ten-quart pail hooked to the housing that covered the well. The handle of the pail was tied in a fisherman's knot to the rope used to lower the pail down into the water, 15 to 20 feet below. Once the pail was filled to the top, we'd pull it back up and dump the water into one of the two buckets we had brought from home. Hauling water was usually a chore left to the men or the boys in the house. But if they weren't at home and the water pails were empty, any one of us would take the two buckets and go to the well.

I remember as if it were yesterday the first time I went to the well alone to get water. I had come home from school to an empty house and wanted to wash my hair and take a sponge bath while I had the house to myself. When I went to get water to heat, both water pails were empty. That didn't really bother me. I had helped my brothers carry water from the well plenty of times. I grabbed both pails and headed through the path up to the well.

I had a rude awakening when I lowered the pail down into the well. It wasn't quite as easy as it looked. There was definitely a special knack to get the pail down into the water in the well at just the right angle for it to sink fast and fill with water. Time and again I'd lower the pail and when it got to the water, it would just lay there, floating on top of the water in the bottom of the well. Over and over I'd pull the rope up a few more feet to lift the pail a little higher above the water. Then I tried imitating my brother's quick flick of the wrist that always looked so easy and had worked so successfully for him. Why, wasn't it working for me?!! He'd flick his wrist and the pail would tip on its side and sink.

Finally, after many frustrating tries, I tipped the pail, sunk it and filled it with water. I pulled it up without spilling too much, poured it into one of my buckets and tried again. This time I was successful on my first try and went home carrying two pails of water.

There were times we couldn't use the water from the well because someone in the neighborhood would get careless and leave the cover up. After one of Uncle Jim Perry's cats or a curious skunk fell into the well, it would take a while before the water was fit to use again.

Dad tried digging a well on our land but hit ledge before he could go very deep. Even though he faced the well with rocks, it wasn't really deep enough to get good water. There was no cover to prevent leaves from dropping into the well. The water was always yellow and only good for watering outside plants and flowers. Sometimes we did use it to clean or wash dishes and occasionally, in the warm summer months, we used the well to keep certain foods cool. We'd put the food or beverages into a bucket and lower it down into the water with its attached rope, getting it just deep enough to rest in the cool water without filling up. It didn't keep foods fresh or cold but was a good place for keeping things cool.

This poem was written by our son, Gary Baribeau, following his vacation on Bailey Island and the memorable day we shared at Cedar Island.

Me with great-grandson, Logan Tranchemontagne
(Picture by Granddaughter, Monika Baribeau)

You walk with grace in the sands and waters of our mothers, and their mothers;
You walk with my grandson, as you did with me;
Only now my children are at the age you were,
And my grandson, my age, when you walked with me.

Memories overcome me, memories gathered of the new
Graceful walk, playful smile, and gentle spirit;
Love grows inside of me as I watch you watch him;
Sands of time, endless water plays happily at your feet.

He smiles, you smile... "Memere let me show you..."
The sun shines brightly on your glowing faces;
This place, this family is grounded on this island;
You smile, he smiles... "Logan let me see what you see..."

Surrounded by those that I love and who love me,
On the ground that is holy and sacred to me and mine
Lies my soul, absorbing what is here, what is mine;
Here lies the answers to life's question: Love.

9
Cedar Island Beach

In the summer, every day that the weather was good, Mum would take us to the beach at Cedar Island to go swimming. With our bathing suits on and a towel thrown around our necks we were ready for a day at the beach. We had no idea what sunscreen was back then, and we never wore a hat. We only covered up with a T-shirt in the first days of summer to keep from getting burned. As the summer progressed our skin got darker and our hair got lighter.

A sand pail and shovel were the only playthings we brought to the beach; the rest of our toys were our own special gifts from the sea. Mum would bring the old blanket she had won years before playing Beano at the Topsham Fair. We might bring a bag with a few sandwiches and cookies and sometimes a bottle of soda that we'd put at the water's edge to keep cold.

We walked along the edge of the woods from our house and followed the same well-worn path that generations of our family had walked when going to Water Cove or Cedar Beach. The path took us past Royston ("Boog") and Madelyn Leeman's house where they lived with their kids, Bob and Pam. Quite often Madelyn and the kids would join us for a day at the beach. We'd go on down through the woods past John Lazarro's cottage, pass by the driveway to Water Cove on our left and the Robin Hood Inn on our right. Then we'd veer off to our left and walk down the gravel right-of-way to the beach at Cedar Island.

White's Family Picnic at Cedar Island
In the Foreground: Annie, Ercil & Janet; Marie & Ira White

Cedar Island was a wonderful place to spend the day! As we got older we liked it better at high tide, but it was a fun place to be whether the tide was high or low. Our favorite thing to do when we were little kids was to catch crabs in the small pond that was exposed only at low tide. It was such fun to sit on the big flat rocks in the pond and try to catch the little crabs before they scurried off to hide beneath the seaweed or another rock. We'd pick up the smaller rocks and lift the seaweed to find the crabs. When we found them we were very careful to pick them up as we'd been taught, if we didn't want to get bit. Our captured little green crabs would spend the afternoon in our sand pails filled with ocean water, amongst the rocks, seaweed and periwinkles that we had gathered earlier.

When it was time for us to go home the adults, as well as the children, would go to the pond to sit on the flat dry rocks and wash their feet in the water, warmed from the hot afternoon sun. The very last thing we'd do before leaving the beach at the end of the day was to set our crabs free.

Sunday School Picnic - 1946.
Front to Back: Steve Johnson, Henry Johnson, Jack Perry, Donna Leeman, Bob Stevens,
Janet Freeman, Ralph Johnson, Bill Black, Bump Orr, Jerry Leeman, Sandra Stevens,
Nancy Johnson

When we got a little bigger we'd look for sand dollars that we could always find on the sandbar, still covered with water, between the two ledges that separated Little Cedar Beach from the big beach. We'd dive for the sand dollars or feel for them with our feet, and with a little practice we learned to pick them up with our toes.

Sometimes my brothers, sister and some of the neighborhood kids would all get together and roll a driftwood log, some as big as a telephone pole, down into the water from the upper part of the beach. We'd spend the afternoon hours riding and playing on it out in the water.

Red Cross swimming lessons were offered at Cedar Island and most of us took the classes and got to be pretty good swimmers. Being able to swim gave us a little more freedom on the beach and around the shore. Now we could explore the little island that we could only walk to at low tide. We'd stay out there until the tide started to cover the sand bar. Our families had warned us about the undertow at Cedar Island on the incoming tide, and we'd been told true stories of children who had drowned there over the years. There had been children of Island families and summer visitors who either didn't know it was dangerous

Neighborhood Kids
Front to Back: Wayne, Cliff Baker, Connie
holding Barry Baker, Ira Leeman, Jack Perry &
June Leeman

or didn't respect the danger of the current between the beach and Little Cedar Island on the incoming tide.

I will never forget a beautiful summer day at Cedar Island with my closest friend Nancy Johnson and my two favorite cousins, Ann Freeman and Ercil White. We walked down to the beach from my house that morning, and the tide was low when we got there. Our goal was to spend the whole day swimming and soaking up the sun. The tide was too low for us to swim so we worked on our suntans for awhile and then waded along the shoreline to cross the sandbar over to Little Cedar Island. The girls wanted to go over to the back side of the small island to see what we could find. I showed them how to pick mussels from the ledges there, and we found a few small pieces of driftwood and sea glass that they could bring home for souvenirs.

When the tide started to come in enough to cover the sandbar, we headed back to our spot on the beach. It was time for lunch anyway, and we knew we couldn't go swimming for awhile after we'd eaten. Mother's rule used to be an hour after eating! But, Mother wasn't there…

We did wait awhile and then the four of us swam over to the small beach on the other side. We tried to pick up sand dollars with our toes between the two ledges that separate the big beach and the little one. One of the girls (They'll tell you it was me!) got the bright idea of swimming over to Orr's Island. All four of us were pretty good swimmers, and we convinced one another that it wasn't really that far, even when the tide was high. It was still early in the day, and we felt safe knowing there were still a lot of people on the beach and boats out on the water.

Nancy, Ercil White, Janet & Ann Freeman

We figured we didn't need to hurry and knew if we got tired we could float or do the side stroke. So, off we went.

Our first destination was one of Stanley Baker's dories that he always moored out a good distance from the beach. After that there was nothing to hang onto until we reached the shore in front of the tall red house on Orr's Island! While we were swimming across, a couple of small boats came by to make sure we were all right. I have to say, it was reassuring to know that someone was watching if we ran into trouble. All four of us made it over there and back, and it was uneventful. We're all in our 70s now and still talk about the time we swam from Bailey Island to Orr's Island.

10
Clams, Razor Clams and Mussels

I t was possible for a man and his family to live on an island in Maine, such as Bailey Island, and survive without having regular employment. Our family, as well as many others, did just that! There was always an abundance of fresh fish, clams, mussels or lobsters to feed our family. Most of the Island women would can or preserve foods as they came into season.

My father would walk down to the shore to dig clams at Water Cove or Cedar Island. If the clams were scarce there, he'd take his punt and outboard over to Stover's Cove or out to one of the offshore islands. Mum went along quite often and would dig a fair amount. Carrying their hods full of clams, they'd walk back up the path to our house where they'd shell them out.

I can still see Mum and Dad, on a cold winter afternoon, sitting next to each other on the couch in the living room of our little house with the pages of the *Portland Sunday Telegram* spread out on the floor around them. The hodful of clams Dad brought in from the icy front steps sat on the old newspapers in front of them. With a couple of favorite shelling knives, bowls and an old dish towel to pass back and forth for their hands, they would shell out the clams. After digging in the cold wet flats, they were grateful for the heat coming from the stove in the kitchen and for the warmth and companionship of the work at hand.

After the clams were shelled out Mum might make a batter and fry the clams or grind them in the meat grinder to make fritters or chowder for our supper. If they needed the money and planned to sell the clams, they'd pack them up in nice clean one-quart canning jars and use orange jar rubbers so they wouldn't leak. My brother Gordon and I would take the clams door-to-door selling them for a dollar a quart. We usually sold the clams to relatives or regular customers around the Island.

Vara and Alton Leeman could always be counted on to buy a quart of clams from us. With each sale we had to take a little teasing from Alton. He especially liked to tease me! He usually asked if our father had soaked the clams the night before. If clams were soaked in water overnight, they would swell and you'd get a much higher yield for your day's work. It was a practice clam-diggers used when they were selling to out-of-town restaurants and people they didn't know or care about. It wasn't something locals would do when selling to their own people of the Island.

Unfailingly, Alton would ask me, "Did your father squeeze those bellies or are they right full of grit?" I'd be very serious and polite when I told him, "No, my father did not soak the clams and, yes, he did squeeze all the bellies." Satisfied with my replies, he'd dump the clams out into a Pyrex bowl, and with a twinkle in his eye he'd rinse the jar and give it back to me to bring home along with a dollar bill for the clams.

My parents liked to go to Cedar Island on a drain tide to dig hen clams, or as some folks call them, sea clams. These clams are very large and fun to dig. The only time you could get them at Cedar Island was when the tide was unusually low. They were meaty and had a wonderful flavor when ground and used for fritters or chowder. It only took a few of these clams to make clam chowder.

One day Mum taught us how to dig clams the easy way. It was a beautiful day in the early spring and Mum, Dad, Connie, Wayne and I had gone down to Cedar Island to go clamming. Connie and Wayne were playing on the beach, and I was looking for lucky rocks and sea glass along the shore. Mum and Dad were sitting on the ledge at the head of the beach waiting for the tide to go out a little more before they started to dig clams. Finally, the tide was low enough. With Dad's hip boots rolled down to just below his knees, he walked out across the wet beach carrying his clam hoe and hod. The rest of us were wearing shoes and socks and weren't dressed for walking in the wet sand.

From the upper beach Mum called out to us kids, "Come on you guys, let's go over to Little Cedar Island, and I'll show you how I like to dig clams!" We all walked across the sandbar and climbed up over the ledges. Mum said, "Just watch closely now," as she moved the seaweed back from the ledges with her hoe and commenced to dig in the shallow crevices that she'd exposed. In a very short time her bucket was half full of big white-shelled clams. She let us take turns using the hoe, and we all had a good time without having to dig deep or go out into the muddy clam-flats.

Many fine restaurants serve steamed mussels today, and most consider them a delicacy, but when I was a kid mussels were not a favorite shellfish. I don't remember them ever being served in the local restaurants. We had them often since they were easy to get and were there for the taking. One of the best spots for picking mussels was off the ledges on the backside of Little Cedar Island. Mussels are full and better eating in the early spring while the water is still icy cold. Sometimes we had the mussels fried, but most times used them to make a stew. Mussel stew is very good. It is rich and flavorful and much the same color as lobster stew.

I remember a time when a couple of us kids went over to Stover's Cove to dig clams with our parents. We had gone in the punt and outboard from Water Cove. It was a good low tide, and along with a clam hoe and hod my father had brought along a tin of salt. Shortly after we pulled the punt up on shore he started walking up and down the beach. He would stop every once in awhile and pour a little salt in the rectangular shaped holes in the wet sand. We couldn't figure out what he was trying to do. I called out, "Dad, what are you doing with that salt?" He just laughed and looked like he was enjoying his little secret as he continued to pour salt as he walked down the beach. Mum said, "I don't know what in the world he's doing!" But her dimpled smile and the sparkle in her blue eyes told us different.

"Look," said Gordon, "The clam is trying to get the salt!" We watched in awe as the long fleshy foot reached out of the hole for the salt. Gradually the whole razor clam came out of its hole and lay there on the flat wet sand. Connie said, "Hey, it looks something like the razor Grampy Leeman uses to shave." Gordon grinned and said in a low voice, "It looks like something else to me." We all laughed as we picked the clams up off the beach and put them in our buckets to bring home. Razor clams need to be shelled out and the meat tends to be a little tough. But when put through a meat grinder or a food processor they make a nice stew or chowder.

11

A Cold Night in January

My father left Garrison Point at the north end of Bailey Island in mid-afternoon on January 20, 1948. With his punt and Evinrude motor he was headed over to Harpswell to dig clams at Stover's Cove. It was brutally cold on the water that day, but the sun was bright, and he knew the digging would be good at Stover's. It shouldn't take him long to get a good mess of clams. Before he left the house he told Mum he'd be home before dark.

The clams were plentiful, and he dug longer than he'd planned. The sun had gone down, and it was already getting dark when he loaded the clams into the punt. He pushed his boat offshore and into the water, settled himself in the stern and took a pull on the starter rope. The motor turned over, sputtered and died. He tried a few more times, replaced the old sparkplug with a new one, and it still wouldn't start.

He could feel the temperature dropping, but the water was calm, and he didn't think it would take him long to row back to his mooring at Rock Ovens. He knew the family would be worried when dark came on and he still wasn't there for supper. His gloves were wet and his hands were cold before he started the long row home. As he rowed, his hands ached from the cold, but he continued to row. After awhile they didn't hurt anymore. He was grateful and kept rowing.

Finally, as he was going through the cut in the Bailey Island Bridge he knew he was almost there. He rowed into the little cove where he kept his punt, and when he went to let go of the oars they wouldn't budge. He knew then that his hands were frozen to the oars, and began to cry for help.

Eighty-year old Joe Pitts lived in the little house next to Rock Ovens and had just gone to bed. He heard Dad's cries, got some clothes on, pulled on his boots, and climbed down over the ledges to where my father was. He pulled gently at his hands, but still couldn't release them from the oars. Joe went back up to the house for a kettle of warm water and once again climbed down over the ledges. He poured the warm water over Dad's hands and they came free. Then Joe helped Dad up to where his little Ford coupe was parked in the driveway and drove him home.

It was long past suppertime and we'd all been in bed and asleep for some time when he came through the door. I was scared when I woke up and heard the noises that were coming from my parent's room beneath mine. The walls and floors in our little one-and-a-half story house were thin, and I could hear loud breathing and someone was moaning in pain. Mum had been quiet at supper, and I think we all knew when Dad still wasn't home at bedtime that something must have happened.

Mum was still awake when Dad got undressed and crawled into bed to cuddle her and try to get warm. In a very short time the feeling started to come back into his hands, but he was in unbearable pain. Neither of them knew quite what they should do. It was January 1948 and our house still hadn't been wired for electricity. Mum got up out of bed and lit the kerosene lamp that sat on the stand next to their bed. The heat of the lamp felt good to Dad. Not knowing what else to do, they decided that the heat of the lamp was the best way to thaw out his frozen hands.

Dad held his hands over the glass shade of the lamp for as long as he could stand it and then took them away to blow cigarette smoke on them. As his hands thawed the pain became even worse. Neither of them slept that night, and when the morning finally came and the light sifted into the room just before dawn, they were shocked. Mum said,

"His hands were so swollen and blistered, he looked like he was wearing boxing gloves."

We had no car or phone, so it took awhile that morning before we were able to get someone in the family to bring my mother and father to the Marine Hospital in Portland. He was there for just a short time before they transferred him to the Veteran's Hospital in Togus. While he was in Togus they amputated the distal and middle phalanges of the second and third fingers of his left hand and the distal phalanx of the index finger of his right hand.

January 1, 1948
Year-round residents of Bailey Island – 235
Year-round residents of Orr's Island – 329

January 22, 1948
Philip Albert Freeman froze his hands and is a patient at the Marine Hospital in Portland.

February 12, 1948
Philip Freeman, who is a patient at the Veteran's Hospital at Togus was permitted to spend a weekend with his family here at the island. He was operated on last Friday and is reported improving.

February 12, 1948
A flock of some 50 white snowbirds have made themselves at home here of late. Another testimony to the "old-fashioned winter" we've been enjoying.

12
Winter at the Farm

My father couldn't find work that fall of 1948, so right after Thanksgiving our parents packed up and moved us all to the Freeman Farm in Brunswick for the winter. My Dad got permission from his mother to live at the farm and to cut wood from the farm's wood lot to sell for pulp.

Dad hired Win Davis and his two daughters along with their team of workhorses to haul (skidder-style) full-size limbed trees out of the woods. The Davis' home for the winter months was a small makeshift camp they hauled to the farm and outfitted with a couple of cots and a woodstove. Win was an unusual character as were his daughters who dressed and worked alongside him like a couple of men.

When there was more than enough food to go around my father would sometimes ask Win and his daughters in for lunch, and they sat with us at the table. Dad had always been very particular about teaching us our manners, and I politely tried not to stare at old Win as he slurped his clam chowder. After a loud burp he looked up from his bowl with his grease spattered, one-lens-missing spectacles and asked my mother, "Ma-am, would you put a little more guts in this bowl o' chowdah?"

We had to walk almost three-quarters of a mile from the farm to the mailboxes at the corner of Woodward Point Road and Thomas Point Road each day to catch the school bus. This was my first school bus experience, since we had always walked to school on Bailey Island. Our bus was the only bus of its kind, and it stood out from all the rest. It was an older bright orange model with square corners. Roland Rush, who was a farmer first, owned and drove the bus. He'd pull up to the mailboxes each morning with a big smile and a half-smoked cigar in his mouth. When Roland wasn't using the bus to transport students, he used it to transport the farm animals he'd buy at the livestock auction each week in Richmond. The school bus always had the lingering blended smells of farm life and cigar smoke.

This was the fall of my fifth-grade year, and I went to the Longfellow School in Brunswick. I went from a classroom of mixed grades and one teacher to a room with all fifth-grade students. It was all very new and different to me, but I made friends, adjusted to the changes and bided my time 'till I could get back to the Island, my friends and all that was familiar to me.

That spring during marble season, which follows Town Meeting and "mud season," a classmate at Longfellow gave me his Quaker Oats box full of marbles. Over the years I've seen Don Reil at our Brunswick High School, "Class of 1956" reunions, and we've laughed together about his gesture of friendship back in 1949.

13
Pyrex Bowls and Creamed Toast

One spring my older brother Gordon and I collected returnable bottles that we'd take down to Joe Lubee's store at Mackerel Cove. The gravel pit was our main source of bottles, but the findings were slim because our cousins managed to shatter any visible glass around the pit while shooting rats.

Food products came in tin cans at that time, but beverages were bottled, and they were the ones we could redeem. We had no other means of earning money and were trying to save enough to buy our mother something special for Mother's Day. There was a set of bowls at Prince's Store on Orr's Island that we knew she'd love, but they were quite expensive.

We picked up a few bottles at a time, and when we had collected enough, we'd bring them down the road to the store and Joe would give us two or three cents for each bottle. After a month or more we finally accumulated enough nickels, dimes and quarters to buy the set of bowls.

With our money in hand, Gordon and I walked to the north end of Bailey Island and crossed the Cribstone Bridge. We went into Prince's Store and looked for the bowls on the shelf behind the cash register. They were still there, and we had saved enough money to buy them. It was a beautiful set of bowls. There were four of them, graduating in size from the smallest blue bowl, to green, then red and all fitting into

Pyrex Bowls from Prince's Store

the big bright yellow bowl. We knew this was going to be the best Mother's Day ever!

When Mum opened the beautifully wrapped box on Mother's Day she had tears in her eyes and cried when we told her how we had earned the money. Our special gift had made her very happy. She loved those bowls and used them all the time. She used the big yellow bowl the most. She found it to be just the right size for mixing up a batch of biscuits, pie crust, doughnuts or her yeast bread. It was a familiar sight to see the yellow bowl filled with yeast bread and covered with a dish towel set to rise on the counter or the back of the stove.

One night she filled the yellow bowl to the top with a lobster and scalloped-potato casserole for supper. After she got it in the oven she started to clean up the sink full of shells from all the short lobsters she'd picked out that afternoon. Gordon and Wayne were doing the evening chores before dark. They'd been outside splitting kindling and carrying in wood to fill the wood-box for the night.

Dad came in with two pails of water from the well up in the field and said, "The guys at the wharf were talking about high winds tonight. I think I'll go down to the shore and check my boat and mooring while there's still enough daylight. I might as well take those lobster shells and throw them overboard, too. It shouldn't take me long. God, supper smells good, Nena!"

Connie and I had just finished setting the table when a loud noise came from out in the kitchen. We all jumped up from where we were sitting in the other room and Mum went right over to the stove. She cried out, "Oh my God, no," as she cautiously opened the oven door.

The beautiful casserole and shattered yellow glass were splattered everywhere. The fire in the wood stove must have been too hot, and the Pyrex bowl with all its contents had exploded in the oven. Much to everyone's dismay, we had creamed toast for supper that night.

Creamed toast was an old standby at our house. Mum always kept a brown paper bag with hard heels

Gordon in the Air Force

of bread, old biscuits, crackers and leftover breads of all kinds under the cupboard. As long as the top of the bag was folded down and kept closed, none of it would get moldy and the contents would keep indefinitely. Everything would just dry out and get hard. It was from this bag that my mother got her bread for bread pudding, stuffing, breadcrumbs and creamed toast.

To make creamed toast she would take a large saucepan and make a thick white sauce of milk, flour and water. After it was smooth and had thickened nicely, she would add broken up pieces of the various breads and crackers from the bread bag. Each of us would be given a generous portion of creamed toast for our lunch or supper, and it was always served with a big spoonful of homemade jam or jelly.

My brother Gordon had been away from home a lot since he graduated from high school and enlisted in the Air Force. When he was home on leave for the first time I thought it would be a good time to fix him a special lunch since the two of us were home alone at noon. I wanted to make him something he might have missed from home and hadn't had in a long time… like creamed toast.

Our Freeman Family – 1953. Gordon holding Connie, Janet, Dad with Wayne & Mum

When I asked Gordon if that sounded good to him, I was really surprised when he said, "Thanks Janet, but unless I'm starving I really don't think I'll ever eat creamed toast again!" I'd always thought Gordon enjoyed our "poor man's meal" as much as I did. Can't remember just what we did eat that day, but it sure wasn't creamed toast!

14
Great-Grandfather
Elisha S. Leeman

Elisha Stephen Leeman was my great-Grandfather, but we all called him Grampy and referred to him as Grampy Leeman. His mother (my great-great grandmother) was Alvira Jane Johnson. She lived in an old Federal style house that set in back of Grampy Leeman's house. It had been built around 1800.

When Alvira Jane Johnson married my great great-grandfather, Thomas C. Leeman, they set up their home in the same house where Alvira had been raised. Their children, Grampy Leeman and his seven siblings, were all raised in that house, too.

When Grampy married Bessie Powell from Cundy's Harbor, he was able to build his own house right next to the Johnson-Leeman house where he had grown up. Grampy Leeman's house was (and still is) on the main road of Bailey Island. Heading south on Route 24, it's on the left just past the Log Cabin Inn and a little before the Bailey Island Cemetery. Grampy was proud to say, "I built this house for $200, and it's all paid for. I don't owe anyone a dime on my house, or anything else, for that matter!"

There are lots of things I remember about Grampy Leeman and that house. Grampy had a big, old, oak roll-top desk in the corner of the living room. It was right next to the door that opened into a hall and the stairway leading to the bedrooms upstairs. There was a built-in china cabinet above the desk that held the good china and glasses that

Grampy Leeman's House

were taken out for company or holiday dinners.

I remember especially the tall frosted water glasses that were kept there. The outside of each glass was painted with stylishly dressed beautiful girls. When the glasses were filled with a beverage and ice the ladies lost all of their clothes, and everyone would laugh! The adults all had great fun with these glasses and didn't think we knew what was going on. But, of course, we did.

An old-fashioned oak wall phone was mounted on the wall next to the roll-top desk. Since it was the only phone in our neighborhood at the time, just about everyone in the neighborhood used it. It had two black bells on the front and a black speaker above the bells. All calls had to go through the switchboard operator on Orr's Island. To get the operator you would turn the handle on the right side of the phone. After lifting the receiver off its hook on the left you would hold it up to your ear and tell the operator the number you wished to call. When you were finished with your call, if it was a long distance call (which most calls were), you could ring the operator and get your exact charges. Grampy always kept a jar on the desktop next to the phone where relatives and neighbors left their coins to pay for their calls.

The kitchen sink at Grampy's was a place of great significance. There were two water buckets on the short sideboard to the left of the old black cast iron sink. The buckets were usually full of water, and they had a dipper floating on the top. A hand pump was mounted on the sideboard at the edge of the sink. Before you could pump water you had to pour a dipper full of water into the opening at the top to prime it. As you poured the water you would move the handle up and down until you felt the pressure build. The pumping would soon bring the water up from its storage place in the cistern of the rock cellar.

The cistern served as a holding tank for rainwater that was collected via a network of drainpipes mounted along the edge of the roof. In the spring there would be a good supply of water, and the cistern would be quite full. But sometimes in the last days of summer the water would get very low and had to be used more sparingly. There was always a metal strainer-type container, about the size of a small soap dish, hanging by its six-inch handles from a nail just above the sink. It held little scrids of soap too small to use for anything else, but when shaken vigorously in a dishpan of hot water it provided enough sudsy water to wash the dishes. The only available hot water came from heating it in a kettle on top of the stove.

The cast iron sink was the only sink in the house and it was used for everything. People washed not only their dishes and themselves, but they also brushed their teeth and got their heads washed in the kitchen sink. These were the days before specialty shampoos for dandruff or modern shampoos with built-in conditioners. When someone had dandruff or dry scalp they used a small double-toothed, fine, black comb to loosen whatever they could before getting shampooed with their head bent over the kitchen sink. After a good soaping, they'd have to contend with half a dozen good dippers full of rinse-water poured over their head while kneeling on a kitchen chair and holding a folded facecloth tightly over their eyes to keep the soapy water out. If you had a score to settle with someone in the family, getting them bent over the sink to wash their hair was a good place to get even.

I have lots of other memories about the time we spent at Grampy Leeman's house. For example, each time we set the table we were reminded to place Grampy Leeman's glass of water to the left of his plate. If we forgot, sure enough, he would always spill it. Whenever we ate meals together he'd always tell us, "If you want to grow up to be as handsome as Ol' Gramp, you'd better eat those raw onions." This didn't worry us too much because we really didn't think Grampy was that handsome, anyway.

No matter who was sitting at his table Grampy usually ended his meal with the removal of his false teeth. First he'd take out his top plate, lick it carefully and put it back in his mouth. Then he'd do the same with his bottom teeth. As kids we thought this was great! Nobody would say anything, and everyone just totally accepted this as something Grampy did!

Grampy had a big old console radio that sat in its place of honor in the northeast corner of the living room. After supper was finished and the dishes were done, it was time for the news and time for everybody to be quiet. Grampy always sat up close to the radio while he listened to the news, and nobody dared to make a sound. If one of us lost control for a minute and started to whisper or giggle, Grampy only had to speak once! His loud "HARK" was a warning we didn't forget that night! Usually there would be complete silence until the evening news was over.

If that didn't work, he mentioned the razor strap that was hanging high up on a hook behind the kitchen stove. Grampy used the leather strap to sharpen his straight razor when he was preparing to shave his silver white beard. Any time the boys acted up or got rowdy and there was too much talking during the news he'd say, "You boys behave or Gramps gonna' use the razor strap on you!" Grampy never got angry with us girls. Everyone in the family knew he was partial to the girls. We could do no wrong!

One of my other memories was cribbage after supper. I loved to watch and listen to Nanny, Grampy, Uncle Jim Perry and Aunt Midie play cribbage together. They'd play almost every night after supper, once cold weather settled in.

Usually Nanny and I would play cards for awhile before Aunt Midie and Uncle Jim Perry arrived. We'd play for toothpicks or pennies. When we played for pennies, I'd bring my winnings home to save in a little jam jar.

When the adults were ready they'd set the card table up close to the parlor stove in the living room where it was nice and warm. I'd pull a stool up close to the card table and watch them play, listening to their 15-2s and 15-4s. If I got tired of sitting with them I'd move over to Grampy's old roll-top desk in the corner. He didn't mind me going through all his treasures, and I enjoyed organizing things in all the different sized drawers and cubbyholes.

Once in awhile on a Saturday, Grampy and I would go to Brunswick on the bus alone. We'd follow the same routine as when we went with Nanny except that before heading back to the bus stop at the end of the afternoon Grampy would bring me to Wilson's Duck-In Hot Dog Stand on Maine Street. At that time it was in the block now occupied by J & J Cleaners. He'd buy me a bottle of chocolate milk and have me sit on the bench inside the small building. Then he'd leave me with Carl Wilson and strict orders to stay right there while Old Gramp goes to the bathroom next door.

I did as I was told and I was an adult before I found out that Grampy's trips to the bathroom were just an excuse to have a quick beer or two at Roland and Andy's bar on the corner. He was diabetic and would abstain when he came with Nanny but enjoyed his infrequent imbibing when he could get away with it!

Grampy Elisha "Lish" Leeman was always a colorful figure on Bailey Island. He was a livery man in his early years and he owned and drove a horse-drawn carriage. He would meet the steamboat each time it came into the wharf on Bailey Island and transport people and their baggage

Leeman's Express Ad in the 1904-05 Casco Bay Directory

from the wharf to the hotels and boarding houses where they might spend a few weeks or an entire summer.

When my great-grandfather Elisha Stephen Leeman was just a young man he served as a cook on a local fishing vessel. This was one of his favorite recipes:

Grampy Leeman's Chocolate Cake

2 eggs	3 cups flour
2 cups sugar	5 heaping T cocoa
2/3 cup lard (I substitute shortening)	
1 t salt	2 t baking soda
1-1/2 cup sour milk	

Blend well – eggs, sugar & shortening.
Add dry ingredients, sour milk and mix well.
(Note: If I don't have sour milk, I sour sweet milk with
1-1/2 T vinegar or lemon juice. It's good to do this beforehand so it can set and sour.)
Just before it goes in the oven, add 1 cup boiling water and
1 teaspoon of vanilla.
Grease and flour a Bundt Pan or an Angel Food Cake Pan.
Bake at 375 for 45-50 minutes.

Peanut Butter Frosting

1 lb confectionery sugar
peanut butter (heaping spoonful)
margarine or shortening (heaping spoonful)
milk (just enough to make a smooth frosting)
add 1 t vanilla
Blend until smooth.

This makes an excellent moist cake that gets even "better and moister" after it has set a few days. However, it doesn't usually last that long.

My mother used to make Grampy Leeman's Chocolate Cake for a special treat on weekends, and she usually made a big jug of homemade chocolate milk to go along with it. Since there

Grampy Leeman on his way to meet the Steamboat at Mackerel Cove.

wasn't always enough money to buy milk from the store or from the milkman who came to the house, we used a lot of powdered milk that none of us really liked. But, by the time Mum made chocolate syrup from water, cocoa and sugar and added it to the chilled instant milk, we couldn't have asked for anything better. Instead of feeling deprived, we felt like we were having something special. (And we were!) Mum always seemed to know how to "make-do."

In the early 1950s when Dennis Baribeau and I were courting, he'd come down from Brunswick to Bailey Island to spend Sunday afternoons with me. Mum usually made a Chocolate Cake on Sundays, and there was always a good supply of chocolate milk to go along with it. I know Dennis came to see me, but I think Grampy Leeman's Chocolate Cake had a strong attraction, too.

In the years that followed, Dennis and I got married, and over a period of ten years we had five daughters and one son. As the girls grew up and learned to cook, he could usually talk one of his daughters into "rustling up" a Grampy Leeman's Chocolate Cake for an evening snack. In anticipation of that first piece of cake, he always tried to talk the girls into frosting the cake before it even had a chance to cool.

Since the 1950s our family of eight has multiplied several times and at last count we had twenty-one grandchildren and nine great-grand-children. From one end of the globe to the other, we've had many family gatherings and celebrations. Without fail, at most of these family occasions, someone in the clan will have lovingly made a Grampy Leeman's Chocolate Cake.

15
Lobstering with 'Lish Leeman

I remember Grampy Leeman's fish house well and my days spent with him on his Hampton boat lobstering. I first remember going out with him to haul his lobster traps in 1946 when I was eight years old and he was 76.

The night before we were going out to haul, I'd stay overnight at Grampy Leeman's house up across the field from where we lived. Gramp would wake me up long before daylight so we'd have plenty of time for a good, hearty breakfast before leaving for our day on the water. We'd sit together at the little oilcloth covered table in the kitchen. I'd

Grampy Leeman's Fishhouse at Water Cove

usually have oatmeal, juice and a biscuit or toast. Grampy would have what I had along with bacon, eggs and maybe even a little fish hash made from whatever was left over from supper the night before. I never could understand how he could eat so much so early in the morning.

After breakfast we'd head for Water Cove by crossing the field between Aunt Mide's and Uncle Jim Perry's barn. We'd walk down Dr. McCarty's road for a ways and then cut off to the left to follow the well-worn path to the springhouse. When we got to the spring we'd usually stop for a minute to get a cold drink of water with the metal cup that hung there for everyone to use. We'd continue down the path through the spruce trees to the fish house on the western side of Water Cove.

When we got to the wharf Gramp would go inside the fish house to get his oars and gear. Then we'd climb down the ladder to get in the punt that was tied there. I'd get settled in the bow, and still standing, Grampy would begin to row the punt with quick, short strokes. In no time we'd be pulling up alongside his boat. We'd climb aboard, tie the punt to the mooring and untie the Hampton. The sun would just be coming up over Ragged Island.

Lobsters usually shed their shells around the first of July. If we were lucky enough to catch a lobster in our haul that day with a "paper-thin" shell from its last molt, Gramp would cook it on the muffler of his boat. We'd eat the fresh broiled lobster with our fingers while we were still on the boat, somewhere out in the middle of Casco Bay. It was delicious and tasted unlike any lobster I've had before or since!

After all the traps had been hauled and baited, we'd head for Mackerel Cove to sell the day's catch. If it was a good day on the water and not too choppy, Gramp would let me take the wheel and steer the boat alone. We'd pull up to the wharf at the head of the cove where he'd unload the lobsters he'd caught that day, buy his bait and gas up for the next day.

Dicer, an Island character and local fisherman, lived in a little house nearby and was usually around the wharf when we'd come in. He was a scruffy, good natured old fellow who loved kids. I always liked it when I saw him at the wharf. He'd come up to Grampy's boat and in that

Elisha Leeman making his approach to Will's Gut with a load of traps he'll repair at his Water Cove Fishhouse.

deep husky voice of his say, "Is that old 'Lish Leeman too darned tight and stingy to give a nice little girl like you a nickel? Well, let me tell you, by gory, old Dicer will give you a nickel so you can run over to Joe Lubee's store and get some candy." Chuckling to himself he'd dig down deep into his old soiled pants pocket 'till he found a nickel to give me.

Hampton Boats

Captain David Perry Sinnett (1843-1913) was a fisherman, boat builder and resident of Bailey Island when, in 1877, at about age 33, he began building a few 2-masted, lap-strake vessels called Hamptons.

In his book *American Small Craft* Howard Chappelle credited Captain Sinnett with building the first vessel ever to use the strip plank method of construction. The design had originated in Hampton, New Hampshire, and these boats were popular with the inshore fishermen of the day.

Source: Harpswell Historical Society Newsletter – Spring 2003

16
Favorite Holidays and Birthdays

Easter

On the night before Easter, after we'd had our supper and the dishes were done, we'd get things ready to color the eggs that Mum had boiled earlier that day. First we'd spread newspapers out on the kitchen table and gather our supplies. If someone had been to Brunswick we'd have an Easter egg coloring kit from Woolworth's. If not, we'd mix food coloring and water in muffin tins. Then we'd use crayons to personalize and decorate each egg with our own unique signature and artwork before dipping them into the pastel waters. After we were finished coloring all of the eggs, we'd set them in a large bowl on the kitchen table. Either that night while we slept or the next morning while we were at church, the Easter Bunny would hide our eggs.

Before going to bed that night we were all shampooed and bathed. Those of us still small enough to fit in the kitchen sink would have our bath and shampoo there. When we got too big for the sink we had to bend over the sink to get our hair washed and then take a "sponge bath." For a sponge bath we'd fill an enamel wash basin with about a quart and a half of warm water and take a bar of Ivory soap, a facecloth and a small towel to the privacy of our room to bathe. We were taught to work our way down from our face, neck and ears, ending with our

Easter 1940 – Dad, Gordon with Bunny & Me

feet that in most cases needed a good soak in the basin before they were washed. Until I was 16 this was my usual shampoo and bath.

(In the summer of 1955 my father's job forced us to move from the only home we'd ever known at the Island to an apartment in a very nice home in Ashland, Massachusetts. This was the very first time our family enjoyed the luxury of a full bathroom.)

Once we were all shiny and clean, our shoes were cleaned and polished and something pretty would be freshly washed and ironed for us to slip into first thing in the morning for the Easter Sunday service at the Union Church on Bailey Island.

The church service seemed to last forever on those Easter mornings! We were too excited to listen to the minister's words or sing the songs of praise with the choir as we usually did. We fidgeted all through the church service until we sensed the end was near. Then we sat very still and listened closely for the familiar words of the benediction. The minister was finally giving us permission to leave the church. To myself I said, "Thank you, Lord, I couldn't have waited another minute to head for home and begin our Easter egg hunt!"

Dad was never one to go to church with us on Sundays so he played the part of the Easter Bunny while we were at church. If the day was warm and the spring grass had dried enough, he would set the colored eggs in small nests he'd make in the grass. He'd also hide the small baskets that he and Mum made from their old egg cartons. They would cut the cartons in half, line them with artificial grass and make handles out of multi-colored pipe cleaners. The little baskets would be filled with malted eggs, jellybeans and yellow and pink marshmallow chicks. I can also remember a couple of Easters that we got live little bunnies and baby chicks! It was a big surprise and a lot of fun.

Easter dinner was always an occasion, but usually just for our immediate family, and it was held at home. We'd almost always have ham scored and stuck with whole cloves and then basted and baked with brown sugar and crushed pineapple. Candied sweet potatoes were a real favorite of my dad's, and if we had them, we'd also have mashed potatoes and other vegetables. Our Easter candy was our desert.

Mayday

About the middle of April we'd start making "May baskets" in our Friday afternoon art class to get ready for May 1st. We'd use small and medium-sized wooden match boxes or make our own boxes from construction paper. Then we'd cover and decorate them with pastel colored crepe paper. In the weeks before May Day we'd start saving our nickels and pennies so we could buy penny candy at Joe Lubee's store to fill our baskets.

When May 1st finally came we'd take our baskets and hang them "on" our favorite people in the neighborhood. I liked hanging my first May basket on Phil Baker, up across the field. He was a favorite person and May first was also his birthday. I'd set the May basket on the threshold by the kitchen door and call out, "May basket on Phil Baker." He would have to come outside and try to catch me.

When we hung May baskets on kids our own age they were supposed to give us a little kiss after they caught us. We would save our most beautifully decorated May baskets with the most and the best candy for a special friend.

As we got older we did things that weren't really very nice! Some of us kids in the neighborhood would take a pretty basket that we had made, fill it with a "cow flap" from one of Uncle Jim Perry's cows out in the field and then hang it on a man who lived down the road from us. This poor man had mental problems and after we set the basket by his door and hollered, "May basket," we'd run away as fast as we could and hide in the bushes. We were scared to death of what he might do if he found us, and I guess that was what made it fun and exciting. But, what a mean thing for us to do! I guess it wouldn't seem quite so bad if we'd filled the basket with candy instead of a cow flap.

Fourth of July

The Fourth of July has always been a time for relatives on my mother's side of the family to get together for a picnic. The tradition started years ago when Great-grandfather Elisha Leeman would treat the family to chowder for the holiday.

He'd bring a big heavy kettle and all the fixings to make fish or clam chowder on the beach at Cedar Island. He'd sit up on the ledges and peel and cut up the potatoes and onions for the chowder. If the tide was right and Grampy decided it was a good year for clam chowder, some of the family would dig and then shell the clams right there at Cedar Island. Others were called on to build a small fireplace of rocks in amongst the ledges. They'd get a fire going right away so it would have time to settle into a nice, slow-burning fire to cook the chowder. Making chowder at the shore and sharing it with his family was Grampy's way of celebrating the Fourth of July. My favorite childhood memories still include the sharing of seafood cooked at the shore with extended family.

Uncle Harold Leeman was a lobster dealer at Mackerel Cove for many years, and every year on the Fourth of July he treated us to lobsters cooked and eaten on the ledges out on the point at Lowell's Cove on Bailey Island. At that time the family was smaller. There would be Aunt Jo and Uncle Harold, their son young Harold, Aunt Rhea, Uncle Ira, Donnie and Ercil, my parents, Gordon, me, Connie and Wayne. There would have been 13 of us and 15 when Nanny Shea and Grampy Leeman were still living.

Over the years our Fourth of July picnic has changed considerably. The biggest change has been the number of people attending. Our numbers have gone from 15 to as many as 100. For many years we were still able to have the picnic on the point at Lowell's Cove. Then Aunt Rhea and Uncle Ira volunteered their lawn and outdoor fireplace on the Hacker Road in Brunswick for a few years. Dennis and I even had it at my family home on Bailey Island the year we lived there for awhile when Lori was born and Debbie was just a toddler. Another year we all got together at Gordon and Judy's place in Dresden. Then for quite a few years Connie and Dana hosted the Fourth at their house on the Harpswell by the Sea Road at Great Island. This is probably the first and earliest memory most of the young people in the family have of our July Fourth picnics.

It finally got to the point where our kids were getting older, and they decided it was time to start taking over the responsibility of organizing and planning the picnic. We had a few very successful Fourths at the Recreation Area on the Navy base and also a few at White's Beach where a lot of us would camp a few days before the Fourth.

In recent years, due to the large number of adults and young children, we've found Thomas Point Beach to be the place of choice. Some years we still try to have lobsters, clams, corn and all the fixings. But there are times that it just doesn't work out, and everyone is told to bring their own food and something to share.

My nephew Jim Freeman would be very upset if his Aunt Connie didn't make the blueberry cake that she's made for years, and we'd all miss the special cookies that Jim's wife Lisa makes for us each year that no one can resist or duplicate. I used to make a fresh peach cheesecake that was a big hit, but it took a lot of time and got to be too much when we were camping before and during the fourth. Lately, I've been making a flag cake or blueberry buckle, and everyone seems to enjoy it just as much. Gordon and Judy still bring the old wooden ice cream bucket and all the ingredients to make homemade grape-nut ice cream that everyone looks forward to each year. We're especially thankful to them and to all those who take their turn with the handle.

Every year at our Fourth of July picnic Jim Freeman brings his Dad's flag and hangs it high in one of the huge pine trees at Thomas Point Beach. (Jim and Donald lost their dad, who was my brother Wayne, in a car accident when he was 30 years old. This same flag had draped Wayne's casket a few years *after* he had survived two tours in Viet Nam.)

2010 July 4th Picnic at Thomas Point Beach – Zack Sharpe, Clayton Parent, Ben Freeman, Clayton Achey, Dennis Baribeau, Ashley Lord, Jared Parent, Ryan Freeman, Kayla Lord, Kyle Graffam, Donnie Freeman, (middle) Alex Sharpe, Jared Parent, Lucas Sharpe, Michaela & Matthew Achey, Travis Jones, Kate Morrissette, Gene Graffam, Matt Brown, (front) Dan Simpson, Michele Achey, Debbie Achey, Joyce Baribeau, Jim & Lisa Freeman, Gordon & Judy Freeman, Dyan Freeman-Taber, Micah, Sabrina & Isaiah Carpenter, Doreen Freeman, Lori & Kristen Graffam, Connie & Stacey Lord, Amanda Jones, Nicole & Emma Graffam, Amy & son, Matt, Janet & Dennis Baribeau

Wayne in USN Uniform

At the end of a day filled with good family fun, shared food and stories, Jim and Donald take the flag down and reverently fold it just right. It always makes me think of my little brother who died too young and Vara Leeman who taught us how to handle our country's flag with respect.

As anyone reading this can see, there have been many variations on how our family has celebrated this special holiday over the years. However, there is one thing that has remained constant. Our family still comes together every year on July Fourth to love each other, share good food, have fun and keep connected to one another.

Thanksgiving

Family Thanksgiving dinners were usually held at Aunt Jo and Uncle Harold Leeman's house at the head of Mackerel Cove on Bailey Island. It was a festive occasion, and Aunt Jo insisted on preparing the whole meal by herself. It was her gift to all of us, and she enjoyed doing it.

She would set the long table in the dining room for fourteen or fifteen people. Aunt Rhea, Uncle Ira, Donnie and Ercil would come to the Island from their home on the Hacker Road in Brunswick. Nanny Shea and Grampy Leeman would always be there and, of course, Aunt Jo, Uncle Harold and their son, young Harold. With the addition of our family of six, the table was full.

The dinner was a traditional New England Thanksgiving dinner which included roasted turkey with bread stuffing, mashed potatoes and gravy, squash, turnip, cranberry sauce and homemade biscuits or yeast rolls. Every year the turkey seemed bigger than the year before. And every year Aunt Jo, an excellent cook and hostess, prepared and

Mum with Deer for Thanksgiving Mincemeat Pie

seasoned the holiday dinner to perfection.

Our Thanksgiving also had another tradition involving Uncle Harold's old gray safe with its combination lock. The safe sat in the far corner of the dining room. Uncle Harold was a lobster dealer who bought lobsters from local fishermen and sold them to out-of-town businesses. He often had a lot of cash on hand. The cash and other valuables were kept in the old gray safe. Uncle Harold liked to tease us kids saying, "If you can open that safe, you can have everything in it!"

We all had visions of one day hitting on the right combination and hearing the "click" of the door opening that would make us rich. On Thanksgiving we had to wait until we were completely finished with our dinner before any of us could take a turn at trying a few combinations that just might unlock the safe. As each of us took our turn, everyone else listened quietly for the "click" that would finally open the door! We all prayed that this would be the day, but hoped it would wait until it was our turn. We never did hit on the right combination, but the anticipation of that possibility was exciting and fun for all of us.

After we finished dinner, all the kids usually went outside to run around the house a few times before desert was served. Our parents said this would settle our dinner enough to make room for desert, but I think the adults just wanted to get rid of us for awhile!

Aunt Jo and our mothers served pumpkin pie and pineapple rice pudding with whipped cream and hot mincemeat pie. It was always traditional in our family to have homemade mincemeat for Thanksgiving. It was made every fall with apples, spices, raisins and venison taken from the neck of a deer. Someone in the family could usually be counted on to come home with a deer during hunting season. A large quantity of mincemeat would be made, then cooked in a canning kettle and preserved in pint and quart canning jars.

Uncle Harold's Mince Meat

3 quarts of ground meat (venison)

6 quarts of apples	1 lb white sugar
2 lbs suet	2 T vinegar
2 lbs brown sugar	3 c molasses
1 quart of cider	1 pint liquid from cooked meat

1 T all-spice

2 T each of cinnamon, nutmeg and salt

Grind and cook venison in a small amount of water. Then strain, saving 1 pint of liquid from the cooked meat. Grind apples and suet. Mix everything together and simmer in a canning kettle until desired thickness is reached. Stir often while simmering and add liquid as needed to prevent sticking to the pan and burning. Spoon into hot sterile jars and seal.

Brunswick Record – November 20, 1951

Mr. and Mrs. Philip Freeman and son, Gordon, just returned from a hunting trip to Stoneham. Gordon bagged a 9-point buck.

November 27, 1951

Mr. and Mrs. Harold Leeman entertained Thanksgiving for Mr. and Mrs. Ira White and family of Brunswick and Mrs. Hattie Shea, Elisha Leeman and the Freeman children.

Wayne, Connie & Janet all dressed up for the Christmas Eve Concert at church. Mum made our taffeta dresses for the occasion.

Christmas

For several years my mother made Christmas wreaths to sell on the Island. Going door to door, we'd take orders in the late fall and deliver the wreaths around the 1st of December. Mum used the money from selling wreaths to do her Christmas shopping.

She always liked to make her wreathes out of fir. There were a lot of spruce trees on Bailey Island, but fir trees were scarce. Most years we were able to get all the fir boughs we needed from a couple of trees next to Grampy Leeman's fish house at Water Cove. Mum would cut the boughs into manageable lengths and wire them around a coat hanger that had been bent to form a circle. After the circle was all filled in with greens, we'd decorate it with the red berries, spruce cones and bayberries that we had gathered from the fields and woods of Bailey Island.

The whole family usually would go to the wood lot on the Freeman Farm to choose and cut our Christmas tree. My father was very particular about getting just the right fir tree. Every year he'd build a Christmas tree stand out of two-by-fours or whatever wood was available. When it was time to set up the tree he'd nail the base of the tree to the stand and haul it into the house. We usually didn't put our tree up or decorate it until the Sunday before Christmas.

Dad always put the star on top of the tree and clipped on the bubble lights that were so special to all of us. After that the tree was ours to finish decorating. First we'd wrap the red and green garland around the tree and then hang the colorful plastic bells, glass balls and the pinecones that we had sprayed with silver and gold paint and sprinkled with glitter. Hanging the tinsel was the most fun of all and was the last thing to go on the tree.

We always had a beautiful Christmas tree. Each year it seemed more beautiful than the year before. The tree has always been the part of Christmas that I enjoy the most! My kids will tell you that every year I'm known to say, "This really is the most beautiful Christmas tree we've ever had!" Then I go out to the kitchen to fix the traditional cups of hot chocolate that we drink with all the lights off except those of the Christmas tree.

Our Sunday School at the Union Church on Bailey Island presented a Christmas concert each year. The children's concert brought everyone on the Island to church, and it brought us together as a community on Christmas Eve. The church was always filled with parents, friends, relatives and neighbors. If you didn't get there right after supper, it was standing room only.

Not long after Thanksgiving our Sunday School teachers started preparing us for the concert. Each of us were given a verse (which we called a piece) to memorize for Christmas Eve. When the big night finally came each child had a chance to stand up in the front of the church and proudly recite their memorized piece. After everyone had finished the recitations, we would sing carols together, and the audience would join us in making it a fun and festive evening for all.

When the concert was coming to an end a tinkling of bells and "Ho-Ho-Ho" announced the arrival of Santa Claus. He entered the church through the door in the back and made his way down the aisle towards the beautifully decorated tree that stood in the front left corner of the church. The angel's wingtips on the very top of the tree gently brushed the high tin ceiling of the church. Beneath the tree and along the lower branches held the beautifully wrapped gifts that Santa would hand out to each of the children.

I remember one very special Christmas when my father was unemployed and money was even more scarce than usual. He hadn't been home much and seemed to be spending a lot of time down to Grampy Leeman's fish house at Water Cove. With the lathes used to build lobster traps he made beautiful doll cribs for Connie and for me that Christmas. He painted each crib with white enamel, and my mother put a decal of little lambs on the headboard of each one. Since I was the oldest, and I'm sure to distinguish one from the other, he made mine a little bigger than Connie's. My mother made bedding for the new cribs and pretty little clothes for our old dolls. Of all the Christmases past I'll always remember the year of the little white cribs. Connie and I treasured the memory of those Christmas gifts long after they were gone.

My father may have been lacking in some areas in his role as a husband and father, but he did bring his own sense of wonder and magic to our holidays. I know that many of the holiday traditions I've passed on to my children and grandchildren came from my parents and the good things that we learned from them.

"The following was not one of our better Christmases:"

Brunswick Record - December 27, 1951

Philip Freeman is a patient at the Marine Hospital in Portland. Freeman was seriously injured on Saturday, December 22nd, while working at the Brunswick quarry at the junction of Rte 123 and Rte 24. He was moved to Portland after receiving emergency treatment at the Brunswick Hospital.

January 3, 1952

Rev. James E. Herrick, Mrs. Philip Freeman and children, Gordon and Janet and Mrs. Joseph Wilson were Christmas visitors at Portland and called upon Mr. Philip Freeman and Mr. Joseph Wilson, both of whom are hospitalized in that city.

February 23, 1952

Philip Freeman who has been a patient at the Marine Hospital in Portland is back at Bailey Island with his family before returning to the hospital for further treatment.

Birthdays

Birthday celebrations were very simple at our house. Mum always made a special birthday cake for us and decorated it with candles and pastel candies that spelled HAPPY BIRTHDAY. Sometimes we would have ice cream to go with the cake, and there was always a birthday gift from our parents.

Since I was born on the day after Christmas, my birthday always came over Christmas vacation. For those kids whose birthdays fell on a school day, each classmate would get a chance to spank the birthday boy or girl with one spank for each year of their age and an extra hard spank to grow on. Some of the boys were pretty rough so it was a good thing there weren't many kids in our school!

Although I never had to endure all the spankings at school, I did have to work really hard to get a little extra attention on my birthday! In the morning while Mum was busy making my cake, I'd walk up across the field to my Grandparents house, and just in case they'd forgotten, I always let them know it was my birthday.

One time I think Nanny had forgotten! As soon as I told her what day it was, she started bustling around and going through all the cubby-holes and little drawers of the roll-top desk in the living-room. She even disappeared for awhile, and then I saw her coming out of Grampy Lee-man's bedroom just off the kitchen. When I got ready to go home, she reached into her apron pocket and pulled out a card for me. I opened it right away. It was a beautiful card with bright spring flowers splashed across the front of it and tucked inside was a crisp new one dollar bill. I thanked her, and she wished me "Happy Birthday" again and, after a big hug, sent me on my way.

As I walked down across the field, I decided to stop at each of my aunts and uncles houses to visit. They invited me in, and I asked each of them if they knew today was my birthday. A couple of them smiled when they gave me their best wishes and put a quarter in my hand as I went out the door.

On another occasion Nanny Shea gave me a birthday party at her house that has always been a special memory. She invited all my friends from school, and the party had all the fixings. There were balloons and crepe paper decorations and party plates and napkins. We played Pin the Tail on the Donkey and musical chairs. All of my friends brought presents, and they all sang as Nanny came into the room carrying the beautiful birthday cake with the candles lit up. Everyone told me I had to make a wish before I could blow out the candles. I kept my wish a secret, and it did come true! It was such a wonderful birthday and one I'll never forget.

17
Outer Islands

⁜

I t was early Saturday morning and all of us kids were still in bed when we heard Dad come in from outside. He was just coming back from Water Cove. There was an early tide that morning, and he'd already dug a bushel of clams and sold them. We were coming down the stairs when we heard him say, "Look, Sis, all we need are a few pots and pans and some food from the cupboards." "But, Phil," Mum said, "We don't even have a tent or sleeping bags for the kids." Dad wasn't about to give up. "Honey, we'll bring quilts and army blankets, and I'll show the kids how to use ferns to make their beds." "And we'll dig a few clams on the island and maybe haul a few lobster traps for tonight's supper."

"Do you think we really can . . . can we . . . can we go camping?" said Connie and Wayne almost at the same time. "We'll help get everything ready," I said. Gordon didn't share our enthusiasm and wasn't too sure he wanted to go on a family camping adventure. He had a few lobster traps out, and it looked like a good day to be on the water. He said, "I think I'll stay home and take Buddy out hauling with me. My traps have been setting for three or four days now and should be right full of lobsters. I can use the money, that's for sure."

Mum said, "I don't know, Phil, it would be fun, and I know the kids would love it, but . . ." Dad said, "No more 'buts' the weather is supposed to be great the next couple of days. Come on, Sis, let's not waste

Gordon & Buddy Out Hauling Traps

any more of this beautiful day talking about it. Let's just get ready and go." He looked at us and said, "Okay you guys, have something to eat and then go upstairs and get yourselves dressed and packed. Put a few things in your pillowcases; grab your quilt off your bed and then bring everything downstairs. We can't bring anymore than we can carry to the shore, so just pack what you really need."

We ran up the stairs singing, "We're going camping, we're going camping!" We got into our clothes as fast as we could, stuffed a few things into our pillowcases, hauled a couple of quilts off the beds and dragged everything downstairs to the kitchen.

Dad and the boys carried things to the wheelbarrow, and Mum packed the wicker backpacks with food as she hummed her happy tune. In a very short time all five of us were ready to set out on a new adventure. I can still see us now, walking "Indian-style" down through the narrow path to Water Cove. Dad had the wheelbarrow full of supplies, and the rest of us followed him carrying our gear.

Once we got to Grampy Leeman's fish house and wharf, we stowed all our camping gear in his small skiff to tow behind our punt out to the island. After everything was loaded we found a place to sit in the punt. Dad started the motor, and we were on our way. When we left

Mum & Dad Heading Out

Connie, Janet & Wayne

Water Cove we headed west passing through Will's Gut and the Bailey Island Bridge on our way to the upper bay.

Over the hum of the motor Dad said, "I think White's Island would be a good place to camp, and it's not far. What do you think, Nena? We dug clams there a while back, and Gordon and I went duck hunting there last year. If I remember right it has a good cove and a nice sandy beach. If there's no one else there, want to try that?" "White's Island sounds good to me, Phil. I do remember all the clams we got over there last fall, and the beach would be perfect for the kids," answered Mum.

A half-hour later we were approaching White's Island. We all scanned the area hoping no one else was camped there. Dad slowly pulled up into the cove and with a smile said, "Looks like we've got our own private island for a few days!" We helped Dad pull the boats up above the high tide watermark on the beach, and watched as he tied the painters to a couple of heavy rocks to secure them. In short order, the five of us had the skiff unloaded, and we were ready to set up our campsite.

Hauling our quilts and makeshift knapsacks behind us, Connie and I climbed up over the ledges to the hillside above the shore to look for a place to make our beds. We found a grassy knoll beneath a thick stand of spruce trees. The ferns were plentiful there. Connie called down to Dad, "Daddy, we found the best place for our bedroom. Will you show us how to make our beds now?" "I'll be right up," he said, "as soon as Mum and I get this fireplace finished, so we can put a pot of coffee on and have a place to cook." Wayne was busy picking up driftwood and piling it beside the rock fireplace Mum and Dad were building.

Connie and I watched the activity below as we cleared our "bedroom" of broken limbs and waited for Dad. There was a good fire going in the fireplace now, and Mum had just put the pot on for boiled coffee. She stayed down below to watch Wayne and the coffee while Dad came up over the ledges to give us a hand.

"You girls chose a good spot for your beds," he said. "This knoll will be soft, and the trees will protect you from the wind that comes in off the water. Now I want to show you how to make mattresses, so your beds will be really soft!"

He took his hunting knife out of the sheath on his belt and started cutting ferns. "Here," he said, "cut it right at the ground and then pile them like this." He grabbed five or six fronds and wove them together, too fast for us to follow. Connie and I watched closer the next few times as he repeated the process. "I think you can do it now," he said as he left us alone with all the ferns he'd cut to see what we could do. We were slow at first, but eventually we got the hang of it. The pile of ferns had been used up, and we had nice plump mattresses.

I woke up early the next morning to the sound and smell of bacon

Dad Fixing Breakfast

that was sizzling in the cast-iron frying pan down below. Connie was all wrapped up in her quilt and sound asleep when I nudged her and whispered, "Connie, wake up. Look, Dad is cooking breakfast over the fire." Connie sat up and rubbed her eyes, "I didn't think he knew how to cook breakfast," she said. We stayed in our cozy beds and watched the beautiful scene below of Dad preparing our breakfast of bacon, toast and "sunny side up" eggs over the open fire. We stayed in bed until he called us, "Okay guys, time to roll out. Come and get it, while it's hot!"

We dressed for the day in our bathing suits and sat on the ledges eating our wonderful breakfast. Mum was sitting by the fire

Mum Cooking Supper

enjoying her morning coffee and a break from her life of being the chief cook and bottle washer! Dad was still busy making more toast to go with the bacon and the last four eggs he was cooking for the two of them.

The cold water didn't stop us kids from swimming, and it didn't seem cold at all . . . after we'd been in awhile. There were no clouds in the sky that day, and the sun warmed and dried our bathing suits, towels and us. We spent a good part of the morning on the beach and swimming. After we had our lunch, Mum and Dad thought it might be fun to explore the island.

Luckily we had changed into our jeans, sweatshirts and sneakers before we started out on our afternoon hike. At first we followed the shoreline and had fun beach-combing. I found a big hunk of red sea-glass, to die for, and a mermaid's purse. Connie and Wayne were both dragging lobster buoys that they'd found up on the ledges next to half a dozen smashed up traps. Mum said, "Let's leave the shore for awhile and see what's up above."

We climbed up over the ledges and as we rounded the next bend we could see where a swathe of trees had been cut through the woods. The cleared trees had opened the land up to the sky and the warm sun. There amongst the slash and cuttings we came upon the most beautiful raspberry bushes. They were everywhere, and their branches drooped

Connie, Mum, Me & Wayne enjoying our lobsters.

from the weight of the ripe red berries.

Mum said, "I don't think I've ever seen so many raspberries. We have to pick, but we don't have anything to put them in." Dad said, "Wayne and I'll go back to the campsite for some containers. We haven't come too far, so it shouldn't take long."

While everyone was figuring out what they should do, Connie and I went off and picked raspberries and ate all that we picked.

That afternoon and the next day we filled every container we'd brought from home with raspberries. Mum said, "After everyone gets their fill of eating them fresh and I do some baking and make jam, we should still have enough to share with some of the neighbors."

I'll never forget the special closeness we shared with my father during the two days and nights we camped at White's Island. Years later my mother would say, "You know, your father was always happiest and at his best, in nature." I agree and think that might hold true for all of us!

We went on another camping adventure either that year or the next. This time we had a three-day weekend in August, and Gordon joined the rest of the family to camp at High Head on the northeastern shore of Harpswell. During our second day serious thunderheads gathered on the western horizon in the late afternoon. The sky was as dark as the inside of a pocket when Mum and Dad quickly filled the wicker backpacks with a few necessary supplies, and the six of us went looking for a safe place to wait out the storm.

Thunder and lightning were all around us, and the rain was coming down in torrents when Dad, who was up ahead, hollered, "Gordon, Nena, grab the kids and run for the barn!" We did as we were told and never did find out if anyone lived in the farmhouse down the road from the barn. We just made ourselves at home and were thankful for the shelter and the dry comfortable night we had in the hayloft of the barn.

Many Bailey and Orr's Island families

Mum picking out crabs at home with Aunt Shirley observing.

would get together on a Sunday or holiday weekend and row or motor out to Pond or Ragged Island to spend the day and have an old-fashioned lobster bake on the ledges. Our family enjoyed many holiday lobster bakes and picnics out on the islands with our aunts, uncles and cousins.

One spring we went out to Pond Island when the baby seagulls were hatching. There were eggs in various stages all over the island, and the ledges were white with gull guano. The seagulls made it very clear that we were not welcome on Pond Island that day. They flew low and circled above us making so much noise you couldn't hear yourself or anyone else talk. It didn't take us long to get into the boat and head for home. We were disappointed that we had to cut our day short, but were thrilled with the fuzzy little baby seagull we brought home with us that day.

On the boat ride back to Water Cove we decided to name our new little pet, Humphrey. We used a wooden lathe lobster trap out back of our house for his pen and fed him broken up pieces of bread in milk. Humphrey stayed with us until he became an adult seagull, and even after he had flown away he'd come back to see us once in awhile. He usually came to visit when Mum was picking out crabmeat. He liked to perch on the edge of her table out under the birch trees where it was always shady and cool.

Dad kept Mum supplied with crabs and built her a special crab-picking table that he connected to a couple of living birch trees. The table had a chute leading to a bushel basket beneath the table. Mum picked out a lot of crabs on that table and tossed a lot of shells down that chute.

When she had finished picking crabs for the day Dad would take the basket to the shore and dump the shells overboard. Our mother's hand-picked crabmeat was in demand at all the local restaurants, and she was able to earn quite a bit of extra money during the season.

18
Orr's Island Grammar School

After the town of Harpswell consolidated the Orr's and Bailey Island Schools, the lower grades from both Islands attended the school on Bailey Island, and the upper grades went to Orr's Island. I entered the fifth grade and started my first year at the Orr's Island Grammar School in the fall of 1948. My brother Gordon said, "I'm not sure, but I think our class of 1948 was the first time Bailey and Orr's Island kids graduated from the eighth grade together."

Mr. and Mrs. Dean Murch brought their love for theatre with them when they came to teach at the Orr's Island School. During the next few years we put on three very successful plays. This was my first exposure to drama, and I loved it. Everyone worked really hard together

Orr's Island School after major renovations.

1947 School Picture: Front to Back - L to R – Patty Catlin, Rachael Baker, Polly Lee-man, Larry Johnson, Steve Johnson, Bill Coombs, Phyllis Johnson, Maureen Murray, Althea Dunlap, Bob Johnson, Jackie Williams, Ralph Johnson, Lucien Johnson, Pete Stilphen, Donna Dudley, Jeff Johnson, June Leeman, Byron Shea, Bill Black, Sally Murray, Jack Perry

1949 School Picture, Grades 6 & 7 – Front to Back – L to R – Edwin Dunlap, Richard Crowe, Wayne Johnson, Nancy Johnson, Sandra Williams, Shirley Shea, Judy Harris, Sandra Stevens, Donna Leeman, Janet Freeman, Glennis Reid, Madelyn Stilphen, Joseph Orr, Al Perry, Mr. Dean Murch, Robert Stevens, Russell Wilson, Jerry Leeman

1949 School Picture, Grade 8 – Front to Back – L to R – Lorraine Snow, Lucille Snow, Yvonne Sylvester, Denise Beaulieu, Alice Herrick, Mary Crowley, Patricia Shea, Donald Rogers, Ruth Johnson, Carol Thurston, Mr. Dean Murch, Doreen Cotter, Evelyn Moody, William Dunlap

memorizing their lines, designing and building sets, and putting costumes together. After the hours of practice came to an end and the initial stage fright of opening night had passed, we discovered the wonder of being center stage and the pleasure we got from hearing the laughter and applause of the audience when we got our lines and timing just right!

The money we earned from our plays was used to buy athletic equipment for the school and to help finance our annual "School Ride" in the spring. The School Ride was an out-of-town field trip that we all looked forward to from one year to the next.

Brunswick Record – January 12, 1950

"The Galloping Ghost," an operetta by Ira B. Wilson, will be presented Friday and Saturday nights at Red Men's Hall by the pupils of the Orr's Island School.

Tickets are sixty cents for adults and thirty cents for children.

Dancing will follow the Saturday show. Refreshments will be on sale Saturday only. Members of the Orr's-Bailey Island PTA will assist with the refreshments. Proceeds will be used for the purchase of athletic equipment for the school.

January 19, 1950

Although more than $100 was taken in at the recent two evening performances of "The Galloping Ghost," Dean Murch reports that only $57 was cleared. Expenses were heavy due to taxes and royalties. However, the sum cleared has been added to a small amount left over from last year and will be used this spring to purchase athletic equipment for the Orr's Island School.

January 26, 1950

The following pupils from the Orr's Island Grammar School made the honor roll: Doreen Cotter, Janet Freeman, Alice Herrick, Ruth V. Johnson, Don Rogers and Yvonne Sylvester.

March 9, 1950

Heating arrangements at the Orr's Island School are inadequate in severe weather, if there is also a stiff breeze. Last week, for three consecutive days, the teachers were forced to dismiss the pupils early because classrooms were so cold.

March 17, 1950

"The Wearing of the Green" was presented at Red Men's Hall to celebrate St. Patrick's Day and was enjoyed by all. The operetta was written and directed by Mr. and Mrs. Dean Murch, teachers at the Orr's Island School. The hall was crowded to capacity for the production.

April 19, 1951

The "Teenagers Club" meets on Fridays at the Orr's Island Fire Hall. Pat Shea is president and Ruth Johnson presides in Pat's absence. Mothers chaperone and provide refreshments.

The teens have recently solicited items for an upcoming Auction. Their goal is to raise enough money to purchase a victrola so they can have dances at the hall.

Spelling was always my favorite subject in elementary school. It all started in my first years at the Bailey Island School when our teacher, Vara Leeman, held spelling bees every Friday afternoon. When I was in the seventh grade at Orr's Island I entered a spelling contest for our school and won first place. From there I went on to compete with the winners from the Cranberry Horn School at Cundy's Harbor and the West Harpswell School. Once again, I won and felt like a celebrity when I saw my name in the newspaper.

Brunswick Record – April 1951
"Janet Freeman, Top Harpswell Speller"

On May 7, 1951, I had to compete in School District 14 in Freeport and came in fourth. After spelling some really difficult words, I misspelled the word "elevator"!

Brunswick Record – May 1951
"The Absent-Minded Professor," a 3-Act Comedy was presented last week at Red Men's Hall to raise money for the annual "School Ride." The play was coached by Louis Bernard, grammar school teacher and proved to be a dramatic as well as a financial success. Jerry Leeman played the Absent-Minded Professor and Shirley Shea, his wife.

They were assisted by the following cast:

Richard Crowe, Janet Freeman, Judith Harris, Nancy Johnson, Donna Leeman, Ronald Mowat, Glennis Reid, Sandra Stevens, Sandra Williams and Russell Wilson.

Ushers were: Mary Hersey, Olive Johnson, Shirley Stilphen and Barbara Williams.

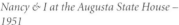

Nancy & I at the Augusta State House –
1951

Shirley Shea, Joseph ("Bump") Orr, Jerry
Leeman & Donna Leeman

Proceeds from our spring play went towards our annual "School Ride" for grades four through eight. Our trip included a short visit to the State House in Augusta, and then on to the Island Park on the Augusta-Winthrop Road for an afternoon picnic and fishing.

In the fall of my seventh-grade year at the Orr's Island Grammar School we started a club and named it the Live Wire Club. At our November meeting we voted to have a school newspaper and hoped to raise some money selling them.

We called the newspaper "OIGS" (short for Orr's Island Grammar School). Each edition was made up of school news, gossip, jokes, a poem, short story, mystery students to identify, movie and song of the week and a notice of upcoming events in school. I was the editor and took great pride in my position! The newspaper was typed on half of an 8-1/2 x 11 sheet of paper, mimeographed, folded in half and stapled to form a slim booklet.

The following excerpts were taken from a copy of "OIGS" that I still have in my old scrapbook:

School News

There were absences last week. Names and numbers of days absent: Arthur Johnson 2, Jeffrey Johnson 1-1/2, Nancy Johnson 1, Jacky Perry

3, and Madelyn Stilphen 1.

Shirley Stilphen has left us and is now going to Cranberry Horn School. She left last Wednesday.

Movie and Song of the Week
The movie of the week was the "Blue Veil." Jane Wyman was the star in this movie, and we hope she wins the Academy Award for her great acting.

The song of the week is, "It's No Sin." I have heard reports around the school that the kid's favorite singers of this song are: Perry Como, Louis Armstrong and The Four Aces.

Jokes
"Darling," the mother asked her small-fry, "Why are you making faces at your bulldog?" "Well," the child defended himself, "He started it!"

"I see you've given up teaching your wife to drive." "Yes, we had an accident." You did! What happened?" "I told her to release her clutch and she took her hands off the wheel."

ATTENTION!!!
The "Live Wire Club" is having a Christmas party December 21st. We drew names at school to see who we are buying presents for. Each child has a name. We are having the party in the morning. Parents are invited.

POEM
"ARITHMETIC CLASS"
by Mary Hersey
As I sit by the window in arithmetic,
I watch the cars go slowly past.

You wonder why I do not know . . .
It is because I am so slow.
To study, to think, what shall it be?
When they gave out brains
They left out me.
Oh, why do they treat me in such a way?
'Cause I'll be here
'Til I'm old and gray.

Our school newspaper is definitely an indication of how naive we were in the early 1950's!

HARPSWELL EIGHTH GRADE GRADUATION
RED MEN'S HALL
June 14, 1951

GRADUATES:
Dain Allen, Affie Bibber, Shirley Bibber, Keith Brown, Edwin Dunlap, Peter Gaudet, Wayne Johnson, Clinton Matthew, Russell Palmer, Alfred Perry, Glennis Reid, Sandra Williams
CLASS MARSHALL   Joseph Orr
Diplomas were handed out by Supt. Howard Fowlie.

Musical selections were played by pupils of Marcia Skillings:
Pat Shea, Mary Crowley and Ruth Vail Johnson.

A Choral Group under the leadership of Betty Skillings presented three songs. The Choral members were:
Denise Beaulieu, Mary Crowley, Janet Freeman, Judy Harris, Mary Hersey, Nancy Johnson, Ruth V. Johnson, Donna Leeman, Pat Shea, Shirley Shea, Lorraine Snow, Lucille Snow, Sandra Stevens and Yvonne Sylvester.

The 8ᵗʰ Grade class presented their teacher, Louis Bernard, with a cigarette lighter. (*"I thought this was interesting!"*)

A Dance followed the graduation exercises.

Sumner Whitney was our eighth-grade teacher for the 1951-52 school year, and he coached us in the production of "The Midnight Son" that we presented that spring.

Brunswick Record – March 13, 1952

"The Midnight Son" that was to be presented on March 21 at Red Men's Hall on Orr's Island has been postponed to April. The following pupils from the Orr's Island Grammar School are in the cast:

Nancy Johnson, Jerry Leeman, Janet Freeman, Donna Leeman, Clifford Johnson, Sandra Stevens, Richard Crowe, Shirley Shea, Judy Harris, Barbara Williams, Mary Hersey, Lee Theberge, Olive Johnson, Madelyn Stilphen and Russell Theberge.

Proceeds from the show will go towards the annual "School Ride." This year's trip will be a chartered trip to Boston.

April 3, 1952

"Midnight Son," a 3-Act Comedy Farce will be presented at Red Men's Hall on Orr's Island at 8:00 PM on Friday.

Admission—Adults sixty-five cents—Children thirty-five cents.

Sumner Whitney, Grammar Room teacher at the Orr's Island School, who has coached the play, announces pupils have been busy all week making scenery and tending to last minute details.

Jones Orchestra will play for round and square dances following the show.

April 3, 1952

Donna Leeman is the Champion Speller at the Orr's Island School. Nancy Johnson came in 2nd and Jack Perry 3rd.

April 10, 1952

Betty Palmer, Top Harpswell Speller. Nancy Johnson came in 2nd and Donna Leeman 3rd.

Left: Me 8th Grade Banquet. Right: 1952 Harpswell's 8th Grade Graduation at Merriconeag Grange, Harpswell Neck – Nancy Johnson, Shirley Dodge, Janet Freeman, Mabel Dunning, Melinda Bradley, Madelyn Stilphen, Donna Leeman, Sandra Stevens, (peeking out from back are Shirley Shea, Joyce Worrey, Mabel Dunning & Judy Harris

May 1, 1952

Pupils of Orr's Island School over 10 years of age will go to Boston on Friday. A chartered bus will leave the Islands at 6:00 am with Mr. and Mrs. Sumner Whitney and several parents as chaperones. At Boston they will visit the Christian Science Building and Publishing House, the Agassiz Museum and the new Science Park.

Funds for the trip were raised by the production of "The Midnight Son" and a public supper.

June 1952

A Banquet for Harpswell's Elementary School Graduates was held at the Red Men's Hall. It was sponsored jointly by the Orr's-Bailey and Great Island PTA.

I graduated from the eighth grade class of Orr's Island on June 10, 1952 at the Merriconeag Grange Hall in North Harpswell. Our graduating class was made up of kids from Orr's and Bailey Island, Cranberry Horn and West Harpswell Schools.

My cousin Shirley Shea and I were chosen to write and deliver a

HARPSWELL GRAMMAR SCHOOLS GRADUATION
MERRICONEAG GRANGE HALL – JUNE 10, 1952 – 8:00 PM PROGRAM

Processional

Invocation	Rev. Harold Coleman
Out Yonder – Original Poem by Miss Lucy Hinds	Elizabeth Palmer
Piano Solos: Beethoven's Moonlight Sonata	Judith Harris
The Spring Song	Nancy Johnson
Old Buildings	Joyce Worrey
Shipbuilding	W. Scottie Armstrong
Soldiers Chorus	Great Island Pupils
Harriet Beecher Stowe	Janet Freeman
Piano Solos: (The Fairies' Harp) Spanish Siesta	Sandra Stevens
Skaters in the Moonlight	Donna Leeman
Elijah Kellogg	Shirley Shea
Legends of Harpswell	Jack Dunning
Presentation of Diplomas	Supt. Hamilton Grant
Benediction	Rev. Harold Coleman

GRADUATES

West Harpswell School – Elizabeth Palmer, William S. Armstrong, Wesley O. Hurst

Orr's Island School – Madeline Ruth Stilphen, Sandra Louise Stevens, Donna Elden Leeman, Judith Harris, Shirley Anne Shea, Janet Freeman, Richard Crowe, Nancy Orr Johnson, Jerry Shea Leeman

Cranberry Horn School – Melinda Geraldine Bradley, Mabel L. Dunning, Jack F. Dunning, Shirley Janette Dodge, Joyce Alma Worrey

CLASS MARSHAL – JOYCE WORREY

1952 Graduation Program

speech to our classmates and their families for graduation night. Shirley chose Elijah Kellogg for her speech, and I chose Harriet Beecher Stowe. I was especially interested in Mrs. Stowe when I discovered that she had once lived on Orr's Island and had written The Pearl of Orr's Island that was published in 1862.

```
"1952"        GRADUATION SPEECH        "1952"

              HARRIET BEECHER STOWE

     Harriet Elizabeth Beecher, was one of Maine's
most outstanding writers. She was born June 14,
1811 in Litchfield, Conn. She attended Litch-
field Academy and in 1824 started school at Har
ford, Conn. a school which was established by
her sister, Catherine. In 1832 she became a tea
cher in the Western Female Institute which Cath
erine founded in Cinncinati. She then Began to
do some writing and contributed a large number
of pieces to newspapers. In 1836 she became a
wife to Calvin Stowe, a professor in the Theol-
ogical Seminary at Cinncinati. For a number of
years after her marriage, her time was taken up
with the care of six childrenand struggle again
st poverty and she found little oportunity for
writing. However through the years 1852 through
1863 the family prospects improved considerably.
Calvin sStowe her husband was appointed to Bow-
doin College, Brunswick, Me. and then to the
Theological Seminary in Andover, Mass. Mrs.
Stowe improved in health, and with more leisure
was aroused to new literary activity by the pas
sage of the Fugitive Slave Act, in 1850, which
was a law made so as, it was illegal to harbor
runaway slaves. She celebrated by her anti-nove
"Uncle Tom's Cabin". It appeared in 1852. With-
in a short time, her book was dramatized and t/
translated into several foreign languages. Afte
the Civil War, Mrs. Stowe bought a plantation
at Mandarin, Florida intending to help the Neg-
roes who were migrating to that state. Although
her idea was unsuccessful. She continued to
live there and in Hartford, Conn. for the rest
of her life. She produced a number of novels
and stories descriptive of New England life.
One of which was the "PEARL OF ORR'S ISLAND".

                   (THE END)


                            Janet Freeman
```

My Graduation Speech

It wasn't until years later that I came across a clipping and picture of Charles Black while rummaging through a pile of newspaper clippings at the Maine Historical Society in Portland and found that Harriet Beecher Stowe had fashioned her Captain Kittredge in <u>The Pearl of Orr's Island</u> after Charles Black, who was an ancestor of mine.

19
The Towers of World War II

W hen we got old enough to freely roam the Island we loved to go to the south end and go into the spruce woods to the old towers that were used by the Navy during World War II. We always thought one of the towers was taller than the other, but found as we got older this wasn't so. They were both the same height, only one was set on lower ground and from a distance appeared to be shorter.

Aerial View of Two Towers – (photographer unknown)

It was a beautiful spring day, and after a long winter my friend Nancy and I were happy just to be out trekking along the shore looking for whatever treasures the harsh winds and high tides of winter had brought in from the sea. Nancy and I had each found a few mermaid's purses, pieces of pastel colored sea glass and a few lucky rocks. We started out from Cedar Island at low tide and planned to follow the shore to Land's End, jumping the big flat rocks that always seemed to be spaced just right so you could go from one to the next.

At the "Giant Stairs" we noticed the tide was getting a little too high to keep following the shore so we decided to cross over to the western side of the Island and check out the old towers. As soon as we turned off the main road, "No Trespassing" signs were everywhere. When we got closer to the towers we could see that the doors were all boarded up. Nancy and I were really disappointed to think we might not be able to get inside. We'd gotten each other all psyched up on the walk in and weren't quite ready to give up on the idea.

After checking it out, we thought we just might be able to squeeze through the narrow window on the bottom if we were able to reach it. There was an old stump nearby that we rolled over and set beneath the window. I tried it first and was able to pull myself up enough to climb inside. Nancy was right behind me, and just like that, we were inside the cold, damp, dark tower.

In the darkness we felt our way to the circular stairs and, being a little nervous and scared, started laughing and running up the stairs, around and around 'till we got to the very top. When we finally stopped and were quiet for a few minutes we thought we could hear a car coming up the dirt road. We listened and sure enough, it was the unmistakable sound of tires on gravel, and it was getting closer by the minute!

Being very careful not to be seen or heard, we peeked out the top window and looked down. The town Sheriff, Sam Doughty, was just pulling up in his big old sedan. Sam was a big man! He stepped out of the car, stretched his long legs and looking up to the top of the tower hollered, "You kids better get down from there right now!" We almost wet our pants!

We whispered to each other and decided if we didn't move or make a sound, there was no way he could be sure we were there. So we waited and we listened. After awhile we heard Sam open his car door and slam it shut. He started the engine, and we could hear his tires crunching down the gravel road and taking him further away from us and the tower.

We were very quiet and listened some more. All either of us could hear were our own pounding hearts, so we figured now was the time to make a run for it. We didn't think this was fun anymore, and neither of us was laughing as we ran down and around those twisting stairs.

I was half way out the tiny window opening, feet first, when I heard the car approaching. Too late! I was caught! I jumped down onto the stump just as Sam drove up and pulled his long body out of the car. Nancy came out right behind me. We both knew we were in big trouble, and we were scared to death!

Sam was gruff and tough and told us in no uncertain terms that it was a serious offense to trespass on federal property. He also made it very clear that by hiding and not responding when he called out to us, we'd made it even worse. He agreed to let it pass this time, but threatened severe punishment if we ever came near the towers again and he found out about it.

Our harmless little adventure had turned into more than we'd bargained for that day. I guess we did learn to take "No Trespassing" and "Private Property" signs a bit more serious and came to realize they are usually there for a reason . . . many times for our own safety.

Years later whenever Nancy or I would see Sam Doughty his eyes would sparkle and a big grin would spread across his aging face as soon as he recognized us. He'd chuckle and ask, "Weren't you one of those little girls I caught up in the tower that time?" Sam got the biggest kick out of tricking us into coming down. He knew all he had to do was drive out to the end of the road, allow us enough time to feel safe again and he'd come back and catch us!

20
Summer Jobs

I was 12 years old when I finished the seventh grade at the Orr's Island School in June of 1951. That summer I worked for Thelma and Parker Luckey on Bailey Island. Thelma's father, George Leeman, and my great-grandfather Elisha Leeman were brothers. The Luckeys lived in Patterson, New Jersey, but summered on Bailey Island where Thelma was born and raised.

I was hired to go to the Luckey's home in the late afternoon to help with the preparation of dinner, set the table and help clear and do the dishes afterwards. They paid me $15 a week. Their meals were simple, and Parker chose to have coffee Jello every night for dessert. As a young girl I thought this was a little strange and might be why some of the Island people said Parker was a bit eccentric and set in his ways.

They had a gray, antique Packard convertible touring car that they used when they went to Portland on shopping trips. During the time I was working for them, they were planning a trip to Portland and asked if I'd like to go with them. I was thrilled at the prospect of a trip to the big city, and my parents said I could go.

A few days later the three of us were on our way to Portland in their touring car. Parker drove along with a big fat cigar in his mouth, and Thelma sat on the passenger side in the front. I had the big plush back seat of the convertible all to myself and had to keep pinching myself to make sure it wasn't all a dream!

When we arrived in Portland Parker checked us into the Eastland Hotel where they were frequent guests. It was right in the middle of downtown and one of the best hotels in the city. They had reserved two adjoining rooms. For the first time in my life, I had a room and a full bathroom of my own. (You have to remember. . . at this point in my life I still shared a three-quarter size bed with my little sister Connie, and we still had no bathroom or running water at home!)

While we were in Portland we ate all our meals in the various restaurants of the Eastland Hotel. I brought home a menu from each of the restaurants and still have them in my old scrapbook. Thelma and I did some shopping, and she introduced me to the junior department at Porteous, Mitchell and Braun. She helped me choose and try on bathing suits and summer outfits. We finally decided on a beautiful salmon colored one-piece bathing suit and a coordinated denim skirt, blouse and shorts outfit which they bought for me as a gift. I'll always remember the kindness and generosity of the Luckeys and the wonderful two days that were so full of exciting and new experiences.

One summer I worked for the Gardner family who lived on the road to the Giant Stairs. That section of the Island was known as "the pasture" to old-timers. I think the Gardner family I worked for that summer was of the native Bailey Island Gardners. They lived and worked away, but spent the summer months at their cottage on Bailey Island. Mrs. Gardner hired me to come afternoons to help with housework and look after their small children. For four weeks I worked picking beans in the morning and for the Gardners in the afternoon.

Brunswick Record Ad – 1951-52
"Bean Picking"
Kelley Farm in Bowdoinham owned by Ransom Kelley is advertising for: 900 pickers, 64 acres of beans, 4 weeks of employment. Transportation provided from: Harpswell, Brunswick, Topsham, Bowdoinham and Richmond.
Interested in employment, call Mrs. Edna Brooks in Brunswick.
In the fields at 7:00 AM and work 5 hrs.

Paid for each day's work at end of each day in silver dollars
2 cents a pound.
Average per picker is 110 lbs per day.
Beans are shipped to a cannery in Gorham, Maine.

The Kelley Farm in Bowdoinham provided transportation to and from the farm each day. A bus would pick us up on Bailey Island about 6 A.M. We had to be in the field and ready to start picking by 7 A.M. and were supposed to work for five hours. If it had rained the night before or there was a fog or a heavy mist, we had to wait till the plants dried off enough to pick the beans. We were paid 2 cents a pound and paid at the end of each day in silver dollars.

For me the gold at the end of the rainbow was a maroon corduroy skirt that I had seen at Senter's store in Brunswick. I fell in love with the skirt when I first saw it. I had even tried it on, and it fit just right! Mum made most of our clothes, but occasionally we got something new for school in the fall.

Senter's was too expensive for our family and not a store that we shopped in regularly. It was such a big deal for me to shop at Senter's for something I really wanted and to have my own money to pay for it.

Each day I put away the silver dollars I had earned. When the four weeks of bean-picking ended I had saved enough to pay for the skirt and to buy a few other things I needed for school.

Nancy and I took the Ouellette's noon bus to Brunswick on Saturday to do our school shopping. We got off in front of the Town Hall, and the first stop on my list was Senter's. I was so happy to see my special skirt still hanging there on the rack. *Janet Freeman & Nancy Johnson*

(In the 1950's all of the better stores prided themselves on having "orig-inals." They didn't carry a dozen or more of the same item as they do today.) I couldn't believe it was still there and would soon be mine. The silver dollars I counted out to the sales clerk represented 500 pounds of picked beans. When we walked out of the store with my Senter's bag and a permanent smile on my face, I didn't care if I bought another thing all day.

We checked our lists and decided to head for the other end of town. Nancy wanted to get a couple of sleeveless undershirt vests at Brehaut's across from the park. After we'd looked through the undershirts in the store, Nancy asked the clerk for help in finding her size. Trying her best to be tactful, the older lady told her they didn't carry undershirts in her size and that most girls her age usually went into little "training bras." Nancy and I were totally embarrassed and left the store without buying anything!

We walked back down Maine Street and window-shopped along the way. Endicott & Johnson's store and Robert's Shoe Store had their new styles in for fall, and it looked like saddle-shoes would be popular again that year.

When we came to Woolworth's Nancy and I went in and sat up at the counter to have a fifteen-cent root beer float. After we finished our ice-cream sodas, we looked at all the different varieties and colors of candy that you could buy there by the pound, but decided against that. School supplies were fun to look at, and we each bought a loose-leaf notebook with paper and pencils.

After leaving the store we crossed the street so we could see the clock at the top of the Town Hall. Seeing we still had time to spare, we went down to W.T. Grant's to check out the clothing department. Nancy tried on a couple of blouses and found one that she really liked. She paid for it, and we left the store to head for the Town Hall. It was still a little early, but we thought we'd sit on one of the benches in front of the Town Hall and wait for the bus. It was always fun for us to watch all the different types of people walking down Maine Street in Brunswick.

We were almost to the bus stop when I realized I no longer had my

July 1952   by Royal Roo

Sandra, Ruth, Donna, Kim, Nancy, Janet (Louise Coombs)

Girls at Louise Coombs – Sandra, Ruth, Donna, Kim D., Nancy & Janet   (Louise in Back)

Senter's bag. "Oh, my God!" People must've thought we were crazy running frantically down the street on our way to Grant's. We really expected it to be right there in the dressing room, so checked that first and there was nothing. Then we went to the clerk who had helped Nancy and she said, "No, nothing was left in any of the dressing rooms. We're getting ready to close for the day, and I just finished cleaning them out myself." Then she checked with the other clerks in the store and called the office. When she got off the phone she said, "No luck, sorry girls, nothing was turned in." Needless to say, it was a long, sad ride home on the bus that night.

21
Hattie E. L. Shea

M y maternal grandmother, Hattie Leeman Shea, was born of Elisha Stephen Leeman and Bessie Ella Powell Leeman at Bailey Island on March 28, 1898. She attended the Bailey Island School until she was fourteen. In her eighth-grade year she was forced to quit before her graduation to help out at home due to her mother's illness. Her mother had not been well for some time, and since Hattie was the only girl in the family they chose to have her stay at home to clean, cook and look after her sick mother. My mother never remembered her grandmother Bessie with breasts, so we have reason to believe she had breast cancer and a complete mastectomy.

Left: Herbert & Hattie Shea
Above: Front to Back – The Sheas: Julietta holding Joe, Geraldine, Hattie holding Marie, Jeremiah, Herb Linscott & Herb Shea

Shea-Linscott Clambake – 1918. Joe, Marie, Herb, Moses B. Linscott, Jeremiah, Hattie & Julietta (Linscott) Shea

Hattie was only 15 when she married 17-year old Herbert Graham Shea from Orr's Island on November 12, 1913. Herb was the firstborn son of Jeremiah "Judd" Augustus Shea and Julietta Linscott Shea. Herb and Hattie's first child, Marie, was born on June 28, 1914. Before Marie's third birthday, Herbert enrolled in the US Navy. It was during World War I, and he was to serve actively in the USN from April 7, 1917 to November 11, 1918, and then in the reserves until January 21, 1919.

My mother, Celina Mae Shea, was born April 15, 1918, and her brother, James Cotter Shea, was born on November 19, 1920. Hattie and Herb's three children were all born on Bailey Island. Herb left his family on July 1, 1922, and according to the divorce decree, continued desertion for three consecutive years. It wasn't until November 12, 1929 that the divorce was finally granted. Herbert was to pay Hattie $12 a week beginning December 7, 1929.

The child support checks were always inconsistent, and Nanny had to find work wherever it was available. Money and work were scarce on the Island, especially in the winter. My mother told us about one winter when she and her mother and her brother Jim lived in a one-room flat in Portland. During that time Marie was living with her father in Salem, Mass. and going to school there.

Nanny had a job with a family in Portland, and the job paid just enough to cover the rent on their second floor apartment. She cleaned for them and prepared their meals. It was my mother's job to look after her little brother when they were not in school. Until Nanny got a second job at the B & M factory, the only food they had was the food Nanny brought home with her at the end of each day. The people she worked for understood her situation and encouraged her to do this.

In the first days of spring she could move her little family back to Bailey Island and find work. There were always summer folks who hired help to get their cottages ready for the season, and sometimes even a few local Island ladies needed help with their wallpapering or cleaning. In the first weeks of May the various hotels, boarding houses, restaurants and cabins would start getting their businesses ready for the summer months, and there was plenty of work to be found on the Island.

My mother told me stories about Nanny washing and ironing clothes for a few affluent summer people in the cottages on the hill past the church on Bailey Island. After the laundry was finished, she'd pack it in my mother's wagon. It was her job to deliver the laundry and bring back the envelope with payment. Mum said, "I was always so afraid the wagon might tip over and ruin all of Mother's hard work. It never happened, but I always worried about it!"

Nanny also worked a few summers in the kitchen at the Willow Cottage on Bailey Island. She peeled vegetables, did dishes and learned a lot about cooking from "Aunt Isabel Johnson." This experience was put to good use when she started her own business at the Rock Ovens restaurant.

Hattie at Rock Ovens

It was shortly after the Cribstone Bridge was completed connecting Bailey Island to Orr's Island in 1928 that Joe Pitts and my grandmother Hattie Shea ran a small seasonal business on the most northeasterly tip of Bailey Island, known as Garrison Point. They cooked lobsters and steamed clams in rock ovens on the ledges next to the shore. Their supply of seafood was kept fresh and close at hand in the lobster crates that floated in the cold water of the cove. It would be picked fresh from the sea, as it was needed and dropped into the pots of boiling seawater.

Customers climbed down over the rocks and ledges to buy the fresh seafood. Most folks enjoyed sitting on the ledges to eat their lunch as they looked out across Will's Gut to Ragged and Pond Islands.

I've been told the Rock Ovens restaurant was actually founded by Joe Pitts, who was a dear friend of my grandmother.

Joe was born in Nova Scotia and came from Rumford, Maine in 1923 to work as a carpenter, gardener and all around handyman for Dr. Eugene McCarty. The doctor, who was also from Rumford, owned a lot of property on Bailey Island. Dr. McCarty bought the land known as Garrison Point from Charles M. York on April 30, 1930. This made me realize that for a few years, Nanny and Joe must have had permission from Charles York to operate their little seafood business on the shore.

We know that Dr. McCarty thought a lot of Joe Pitts and wanted to make it possible for him to eventually buy the land himself. By the doctor's purchase of the property in 1930, Joe and Hattie could continue to run their business, and Joe was able to build a small storage shed up next to the road for their soda and supplies.

The land purchase in 1930 included the original site of the Rock Ovens, the land on which the Bailey Island Motel was built, and the fish house on the shore behind the motel known as "The Shack" or the "Spark Plug."

They continued to cook clams and lobsters down on the ledges in their rock ovens, and the business continued to grow. It took several years before they were finally in a position to buy the land themselves.

On October 25, 1940 Hattie E. Shea and Joseph Pitts received the deed from Eugene McCarty for the property and became equal business partners and good friends until Joe's death on October 16, 1948.

Joe built the first Rock Ovens Restaurant, as shown:

Brunswick Record – September 29, 1938 – Bailey Island News

The Rock Ovens Ice Cream and Shore Dinner Parlor at Garrison

Rock Ovens as it looked in 1940s – 1950s   *Joe Pitts*

Point closed for the season Sunday.

In later years their menu included Full Shore Dinners, Baby Shore Dinners, Fried Clams, Steamed Clams, Clam and Fish Chowders, Lobster Stew, Baked Stuffed Lobsters, Steamed or Boiled Lobster and Fried Lobster (that was called "Lazy Man's Lobster"). The guests enjoyed a wonderful assortment of desserts made with whatever berries and fruits were in season at the time. Old-fashioned puddings, dumplings, pies, cakes and cobblers were all freshly baked at the restaurant each day. The restaurant opened for business on weekends in May and after Memorial Day it was open every day until they closed for the season after Labor Day.

Topsham Fair was always held in October, and every summer while Nanny was working long hours at the Rock Ovens, she anticipated the end of the tourist season and the opening days of the Topsham Fair. She'd go to the Fair every day the weather was good and could usually be found in the Beano tent. Each year she was able to add a couple of new Indian blankets to her chest from her winnings. In the afternoons she liked to sit in the grandstand and watch the horse races. I'm not really sure if she bet on the races or just enjoyed watching them race. Topsham Fair was definitely the event of the year for Nanny. After the death of Joe Pitts in 1948, his heirs sold Joe's share of the business to Eileen and Larry Johnson.

My grandmother was not well during this time. Her weakened physical condition eventually proved too much for her, and shortly after Joe Pitts' death she had a nervous breakdown. The two months she spent at the State Hospital in Augusta helped her, and she was able to come back home, but her days of running the Rock Ovens were over.

My mother Celina Freeman and her "Auntie" Eileen Johnson ran the Rock Ovens the summers of 1949 and 1950. I took care of my little sister Connie, my brother Wayne, and young Larry (or "Little Larry" as we called him) who lived in the small house next to the restaurant where Joe Pitts had lived. These were very different and difficult summers for our family. We were all used to having our mother at home all the time, and now she was gone every day working long hours in the restaurant.

Joe and Hattie Gamache had used or rented the fish house (known as the "Shack" or "Spark Plug") as a summer cottage for as long as I

could remember. They were finally able to purchase it in April of 1949. The Gamaches had a lovely granddaughter, Dottie Pelletier, who came to stay with her grandparents quite often. She and I became very close friends during that time.

In the spring of 1951 Hattie and the family felt they should sell her share of the Rock Ovens and the remaining property. Eileen and Larry Johnson then bought my grandmother's share and took full possession in May of 1951.

Hattie E. (Leeman) Shea – Mother's Day 1951

Brunswick Record – May 17, 1951

Rock Ovens opened last weekend. Mrs.Lawrence Johnson, proprietress. Kitchen: Addie Moody, Edna Shea, Prudence Alexander. Dining Room: Cathryn Leeman and Lois Gott.

Six years later, on March 30, 1957, the Johnsons sold the Rock Ovens to Eileen's nephew, Bruce and his wife Joanne Allen. With the exclusion of the "Sparkplug" the sale included all of the original property that

Joe Pitts and Hattie Shea bought from Dr. McCarty in 1940.

Since the 1950s the Rock Ovens has gone through many changes. In the 1960s the Allens rebuilt the Rock Ovens, updating the appearance with stone, glass and weathered gray shingles. A fire in the winter of 1978 also forced another restoration. Bruce's sister, Sue Favreau, ran the restaurant for several years, and Sumner Whitney and his wife and other family members ran it for a time, as well.

Janet & Selina – Ready for work at Rock Ovens.

Jack Baker also had a successful business there for many years. Everyone missed Jack when he decided to downsize and opened "Jack Baker's Last Stand" next to the Bailey Island Post Office. In 2008 Jack sold his restaurant to Chris and Heather Coffin, and it's now known as the Giant Stairs Seafood Grille. I guess Jack still wasn't quite ready to retire from the restaurant business in 2008. The last I knew he still had a small breakfast and lunch cafe on the main street of Richmond.

The current owners of the Rock Ovens restaurant opened for the 2006 season, but its been closed for the past two summers due to the renovation of the Bailey Island-Orr's Island Bridge. The restored bridge reopened on November 20, 2010.

My Special Memories of Nanny Shea

Hattie holding me.

From my earliest memories Nanny Shea always lived up across the field from us. Her father, Elisha Leeman, set up an apartment for her and her three children shortly after her divorce in 1929. She had a kitchen and living room on the lower level and three bedrooms upstairs. "Lish" and his wife Bessie lived in the main part of the house. In later years, after Bessie passed on and the kids were grown, Hattie moved in and kept house for her father. When the apartment became vacant newlyweds Bea and Phil Baker moved in. They rented the apartment until they were ready to build their house on the land next door.

I loved getting into Nanny's big, deep baking drawer in the white kitchen cupboards. It smelled of spices and chocolate, and I'd sometimes help myself to a few chocolate chips, raisins or dates. Nanny usually kept a good supply of date-filled cookies in the tall red tin with the crystal knob that sat on the counter just above the baking drawer. They weren't the dropped date-filled cookies we make today. They were the old fashioned kind made with white flour and rolled out and cut with a biscuit cutter before being filled with a date and raisin mixture.

It was always a special Saturday when I got to go to Brunswick on the bus with Nanny Shea and Grampy Leeman. Usually I would dust for Nanny on those mornings, and she would pay me twenty-five cents. It was fun to have a little money of my own for the afternoon in Brunswick.

During the summer months Ouellette's bus made two trips to the Island every Saturday. There was no official bus stop. Anyone taking the bus to town could stand out on the main road anywhere and get picked up. We'd wait for the bus right in front of Grampy Leeman's house.

(Sometimes my parents took the bus to do their errands and get groceries. If we needed a new pair of shoes Mum would have us stand on a piece of cardboard and trace around each foot. She'd cut out the outlines and the clerk in the shoe store used them as a guide to select the correct size. It seemed to work quite well.)

When Nanny Shea and I arrived in Brunswick we'd get off the bus at the Town Hall, which stood at the corner of Town Hall Place and Maine Street. (After being demolished during the urban renewal days of the 1960s the Town Hall site became the location for the Grand City department store for many years.) There was usually just enough time for a nice lunch at Jarvis Restaurant, on the corner of Maine and Cumberland Streets, before going to the movies at the Cumberland Theatre next door. In the late 1940s the admission price for someone my age was twelve cents.

After the movies we might do a little shopping from Nanny's small list of things to pick up in town. Then we'd go into Woolworth's and have a cold drink or an ice cream soda before walking back to the bus stop in front of the Town Hall.

When I stayed up across the field at Nanny's, one of my favorite pastimes was going through her button box. It was a colorful tin box filled with buttons of every size, color and description. The box held buttons that my grandmother as well as her mother and grandmother before her had removed from discarded or old worn out clothes. Whenever I'd ask Nanny about an unusual or beautiful button, she'd stop whatever she was doing and sit down with me for awhile. It seems there was always a fascinating story to be told.

One rainy afternoon she showed me how to make a "Whiz Button" with some thread and an oversized winter coat button. This simple little toy was made by looping about 16 inches of strong thread through the holes of a big button and tying both ends of the thread together in a knot. Then, with your index fingers in the loops, you would pull the thread taut and then give it some slack. If you repeated this several times the button would spin and make a "whizzing" sound.

Quite often Nanny would have our family up for supper on Sunday nights. She'd make yeast dough then roll it out and cut it with a doughnut cutter. She fried these dough pieces in deep fat and turned them as you would doughnuts. After they had been fried, she would dip each one individually into a pot of hot molasses to coat it. I've tried to find out what we called them but no one seems to know. "Pig's Backs" is what I remember. Regardless of what they were called, they were very good!

All of us kids loved eating this sticky sweet supper that we only ate at Nanny's while sitting on high stools at the linoleum covered kitchen sideboard. When the two lower cupboard doors were left open our stools fit up to the sideboard just right. This gave us enough room for a couple of extra kids that wouldn't fit at the fold-out table in the kitchen. With the cupboard doors open, I can still see the huge tins of shortening and flour that were stored there as staples for the long winter months.

I slept with my grandmother when I stayed overnight up across the field. The only heat that ever touched the upstairs bedrooms came from one small register in the floor of each room. This allowed a small amount of heat to rise up from the stoves downstairs. In the wintertime Nanny usually brought a hot water bottle to bed with us. She'd wrap it in a towel and put it down to the foot of the bed to keep our feet warm. With the hot water bottle and warm double sheet blankets and home-made quilts, we slept cozy and warm no matter how low the temperature got or how much the northeast wind blew through the eaves of the old house.

My grandmother Hattie Shea died of cancer in the bedroom right off the kitchen in her father's house on July 12, 1952. She died in the same house on Bailey Island where she'd been raised and had spent most of her life. Hattie was 54 years old and had not been well for several years. She suffered from cancer and Bright's disease. Her death certificate stated carcinoma of the right ureter and cervix as the cause of her death.

In the weeks and months prior to her death, my mother and her sister Marie White took care of Nanny in her home. They hired Hazel Dexter to help out occasionally, and Dr. Louis Bachrach drove down to the Island from Brunswick regularly to examine her and adjust her medications.

The day my grandmother died my cousin Ercil and I had picked her a beautiful bouquet of wildflowers and brought them to her room. Her death was an especially traumatic time for me. I'd spent so much time with her over the years and had been with her throughout her long illness.

I was with my grandmother when she started losing touch with reality. One time I'd been there for supper and was spending the night. Her bedroom was on the west side of the house facing the main road, and we had always slept together there in her double bed. That night, as we'd gone upstairs to go to bed, she went into Uncle Jim's room across the hall instead of going into her own bedroom as she usually did.

When I found her she was standing there looking out the window that faced east toward our house, down across the field at the edge of the woods. She was crying softly, "Oh no, oh no." Frightened, I went in behind her to see what could be wrong. I looked out the window and could see nothing but darkness. My grandmother saw fire. She thought all the woods and our house were on fire.

That was the summer of 1948 when I was nine and a half years old. At first I was really scared and didn't know what to do. Then I knew that I had to get some help. During this time Bea and Phil Baker lived in the apartment in the other side of the house, and I could still hear them downstairs. I went down and told them what was happening. Bea came upstairs with me, and Phil went down across the field to get my mother.

Nanny spent a good part of that summer in the Maine General Hospital in Portland. She had a complete hysterectomy and 72 hours of radiation implants to deter the cancer they had found.

During that time she hallucinated and saw fires everywhere. At one point while she was there, she tried to jump out the window of her room because there was a small fire across the street. In time her condition did improve, and she was able to come home. I remember especially how she acted when I first saw her. She hugged me and said, "I hope you're not afraid of your Nanny." And, I wasn't! Her health was not good, but she was home, and I was able to stay overnight with her again.

I stayed over on a Friday night in October of the same year, and early the next morning woke from a sound sleep to a woman screaming right outside our window. It didn't take me long to realize it was Aunt Midie Perry, and she was crying, "It's Joe Pitts, and he's dead." Nanny was still sound asleep, and I thanked God for that. When I got out of bed and looked out the window Aunt Midie was standing there on the corner next to Joe Pitts. He was sprawled face down on the side of the road. My grandmother's friend and business partner of over 20 years had died.

I was not quite ten years old, but had enough sense to know the shock of Joe's sudden death might send Nanny back into the hospital again. I tried to be very quiet when I closed the shades and quietly got back into bed where I snuggled up close to Nanny, and prayed that she'd continue to sleep until all the commotion outside subsided and someone got word to my mother.

Joe Pitts died on October 16, 1948, and Nanny was admitted to the Augusta State Hospital on October 30, 1948, where she was to remain for two months. Hattie E. Shea was fifty years old.

Brunswick Record—October 21, 1948

Joseph Pitts, 80, died suddenly on Saturday, at Bailey Island. He had been in poor health for several months.

Mr. Pitts was born in Nova Scotia on April 16, 1868 of Gertrude (Avery) and Edward Pitts. He came to Bailey Island from Rumford about 1923 and has resided at the island continuously since then. He worked for many years for Dr. E. M. McCarty as a maintenance man and gardener for the Dr.'s properties.

He was co-owner of the Rock Ovens Restaurant on Bailey Island.

His mother, Gertrude Avery, was born in Larry's River, Guy's County, Nova Scotia. Surviving is his sister, Mrs. Lucy DeYoung of Heatherton, N.S. Prayers were said Monday morning at Laws Funeral Home.

Harold Leeman wrote the following letter dated December 1948 to his sister, Hattie, while she was being treated at the State Hospital in Augusta:

Dear Sister,

Just a line to let you know how glad I am that you are getting along so well and that it won't be long before you are coming home again. I am sorry that we didn't get your Christmas presents up to you in time for Christmas but we still have them here and if we get up we will bring them and if not they will be here when you get home.

Dad is staying down here with us for a while and he is feeling fine. Joe,

Harold and Dad have gone to Brunswick this afternoon and I am here alone. I have beat Dad so bad playing cribbage that I expect you can hear him hollering up there sometimes.

We all had a nice Christmas up at Marie's and all got a lot of nice presents and had a nice dinner. The weather is quite bad down here now and boats are not going out very often. Dad is going to stay down here until the first of the week and then he is going up to Marie's again. He has got his boat hauled up and all taken care of and am glad of that because we won't have to worry about it when the wind blows. Aunt Midey and Uncle Jim are coming down to play cribbage with us tonight.

Joe and I went to Portland week before last and stayed three nights but that was not long enough for her to get her Christmas shopping done. You know Joe. Bought her a nice pair of Black Onyx earrings with a small diamond set in them and a new housecoat. The kids all got lots of presents and were real pleased with them. Little Connie and Wayne were some pleased with the things that they got.

We all stayed up to Marie's the night before Christmas and I don't know whether Ercil or Dad was the most anxious to get up in the morning. Harold and Dad slept together and Harold said Dad tried to get him up at four o'clock.

Well, Sis, I think I have written you quite a letter so will have to quit for now. Take care of yourself and it won't be long before you are home again. I think that some of us will be up this week to see you. If not, we will be up the first of next.

Lots of love,
Brother Harold

22
James Cotter Shea

Born: 11-19-1920
Died: 03-11-1965
Body Recovered: 05-16-1965

im Shea was the third child and only boy born to Hattie (Leeman) and Herbert Graham Shea. At the time of his birth he had two older sisters. Marie was six years old, and my mother, Celina, was two. Herbert had been in the US Navy and served in World War I, and he also served with his son, Jim, in World War II.

After the separation of Jim's parents in 1922 he spent most of his early years with his father Herbert at the old family home

Jim Shea in White USN Uniform, his father, Herbert Shea far right

on Little Island. Herb lived there with his parents, Julietta and Jeremiah, several of his brothers and sisters, and his grandfather, Moses B. Linscott.

Uncle Jim played an important part in my life as I was growing up. When he was ashore from whatever fishing dragger he'd been on at the time, he was always around the Island. He would show up at the last minute for a holiday meal, and our house was one of his first stops after

155

a long trip at sea. Without fail he'd come in with a big jug of Seagram's "7" Whiskey in one hand, a bag of fresh whole haddock in the other, and his pockets filled with money from his trip out. Whenever he came into port it was a time to celebrate. Many times he'd walk through the door saying, "Hey Nena, get your boots on and grab a jacket. We're going down the road and have a little drink with ole Dicer." Dicer was an old fellow who lived alone in a little shack at the head of Mackerel Cove.

I remember one time in particular when this happened. I was a young adult, and my mother and I were supposed to go to a shower that night at Lila Baker's house up the road from us. Well, Mum came home after being at Dicer's with Uncle Jim, and she was very inebriated. We all had our supper that night, and she got herself together enough to go, but it was a long painful evening for her.

Sometimes Uncle Jim would come in and say, "Hey, Sis, 'feel like going for a little ride over to Orr's Island? Just around the cove to see if Gene Wilson is home and bring him a drink of whiskey." Or, he'd stop by late afternoon with, "What do you say, Sis, you hungry for a good steak? When Phil gets back from clamming, how about we take a ride into Portland and all have the biggest steak they've got at Valle's. I think we could all use a good steak. How about it?! You go get all prettied up, and I'll be back to pick you guys up around 4:30."

By the time he got back, he sometimes had added a few friends to join them. He stopped to see Mary and Mike Doughty and asked them if they'd like to come. Mike said, "Cwist (Christ) yes, Jimmy, we'd love to go into Valle's with you and Phil and Nena."

If he'd partied too much during his time ashore and needed to get straightened out, he'd come to our house with a big grocery bag filled with canned tomatoes. He believed a big bowl or two of hot stewed tomatoes and lots of rest was the "cure-all" for a bad hangover.

By the time he'd ship out again, he'd have spent all his money. He knew it was time to go back to sea when he could turn his pockets inside-out and all he could find was a lot of lint and a well-used handkerchief.

Uncle Jim loved my mother dearly and in his own way always tried to bring good cheer and happiness into her sometimes very difficult life. Usually whenever there was an atmosphere of a party at our house, it was Uncle Jim who had brought it in with him.

My Nanny Shea had one of those big white electric roasters that were popular in the late 40s. I remember one time in the middle of winter when my parents and Uncle Jim got it in their head to have a "lobster feed"! They got some lobsters together (shorts, I'm sure!) and proceeded to cut the live lobsters down through from the underside of the top of the body to the tip of the tail. Then they spread them open and one by one filled them with the prepared mixture of crushed crackers, crabmeat and melted butter, laying the stuffed lobsters side by side in the bottom of the roaster. As the others were filled, they would layer them until the roaster was filled to the very top. After placing the cover on and turning the dial to the desired temperature, it took about an hour for them to bake. When we got up the next morning all of us kids thoroughly enjoyed having cold left-over baked stuffed lobsters for breakfast!

Uncle Jim joined the Navy early in 1942, a few months after his 21st birthday. He served in Africa and in the Pacific during World War II and saw action aboard a Bath-built destroyer. He was loud in his praise for it. During his time as a member of the destroyer's crew, they witnessed seven Japanese sailors (or "Japs" as they called them in those days) on a life raft taking their own lives rather than be taken prisoners. When they first saw the life raft they thought it contained seven dead bodies. But as they got closer the men sat up. Uncle Jim said when they were about fifty yards off, the officer on the raft whipped out a submachine gun. He and the others watching quickly hit the

James Cotter Shea

deck. At that range the Japanese officer could have cleaned off the bridge in two seconds.

One of the men on the raft was pleading with the officer. The officer barked out an order and two of the men grabbed the protestor and held him by the arms while the officer shot him. One by one all of the other Japanese sailors were shot by the officer. "Then he turned to us," Jim said. "He delivered a harangue which nobody understood and then shot himself."

While Uncle Jim was in the Pacific he met an old friend who was also from Bailey Island. He and Bill Skillings had a great time sharing their news from home. Johnny Murray, another boyhood friend from Bailey Island who grew up and went to school with Jim and Bill Skillings, didn't make it home from the war. The following 1946 Brunswick Record article explains:

Brunswick Record – 1946
Bailey Island Child Receives Father's Posthumous Silver Star

The one-and-a-half-year-old son of Pvt. John L. Murray Jr. receives his father's Silver Star posthumously on Monday. The son he only saw once, received the Silver Star posthumously awarded his father.

John L. Murray III, the son Pvt. John L. Murray only saw once, was presented the medal awarded to Pfc. John L. Murray Jr., formerly of Bailey Island, who was killed in action April 12, 1945. The son received the medal for his mother, Mrs. Julie M. Murray. The award was made by Lt. Charles L. Williamson, Army Recruiting Service.

According to the citation Private Murray distinguished himself March 26, 1945 in the vicinity of Limburg, Germany. His tank and three others were isolated from their unit and the enemy immediately surrounded the tanks and destroyed them, forcing Private Murray and the other crew members to withdraw to a nearby house and set up a defensive position.

"Realizing that his force would soon be annihilated if reinforcements did not arrive, Murray disregarded direct enemy fire and rushed through the enemy lines to the river. Wading across in full view of the enemy, he informed friendly infantry of the situation and led them across the river to aid his comrades."

Murray was the son of the late John L. Murray and Mrs. Helen Murray of Bailey Island. He was educated in the schools at Brunswick and operated his own trucking business on Bailey Island, prior to entering the Army, July 24, 1944. He received his basic training at Fort Devens and trained for overseas at Camp Croft, S.C. He served with the 9th Armored (Infantry) Division, First Army. At the time he saw his son, the baby was but a day old.

Besides his son, others present at the awarding ceremony included his mother, wife, daughter, Sally Lee Murray, aged seven years, and two sisters, Mrs. Louise Coombs and Mrs. Grace Leeman, all of Bailey Island.

Mildred Lane was a very good friend of Uncle Jim's for many years, and our family had always hoped they might get married some day. She was a school teacher from the Lewiston-Auburn area and came to Bailey Island each year to spend the summer at her family's cottage at Oceanside. A marriage between the two never did come about!

Jim Shea gave up his bachelor days shortly after he met and courted Marie Deshon. He had finally met someone who turned his head enough to think of settling down to married life. Marie had two sons, Joseph Peterson and Vincent "Lucky" Oppedisano, when she and Uncle Jim got married.

Marie F. Deshon was born of Maxwell and Iola Liscomb Deshon in Harpswell, Maine on October 10, 1920. She was a graduate of Yarmouth Academy and worked most of her life in various shoe manufacturing plants in the area. When she was young, her father was a lighthouse keeper, and she spent many years on the Maine coast. Marie married Robert J. Hall of Chelsea after Jim's death. She died in Augusta on July 26, 2005.

In 1965 Jim Shea was working for the Snow Canning Company aboard the Fred H. Snow. The boat was tied up at the Pier at Point Pleasant Beach, New Jersey. In the early evening of March 11, 1965 Jim and some of his buddies were having a party aboard the boat. He disappeared that night along with his 1950 Dodge Coupe. Subsequently he was reported missing to the Point Pleasant Beach Police Department. Two months and five days later his body was recovered from the inland waterway known as Manasquan Inlet. The U.S. Coast Guard found his body at 6:51 A.M. on May 16, 1965. Identification was made from his dental records. An autopsy disclosed submersion as the cause of death. An investigation took place, and no indication of foul play was reported.

News Clippings:
N.J. Police Probing Death of Bailey Island Fisherman
Point Pleasant Beach, New Jersey

Authorities here said Tuesday night they could not discuss circumstances surrounding the death of James C. Shea, 44, of Bailey Island, Maine, whose body was recovered Monday in Manasquan Inlet, the inland waterway.

Police officer Jack Trout, who is conducting the investigation with detective Milton Couch of the Point Pleasant Beach Police Department, said the matter is still under investigation. Trout said he hoped the case may be wound up by Wednesday.

As nearly as can be determined, Shea, who had been employed by the Snow Canning Factory at Point Pleasant Beach, has been missing since March 11.

Trout said that was an approximate date. But he said he could not say whether Shea died by drowning. Nor would he comment one way or another when asked if an autopsy had been performed.

Shea's body was released to members of the family Tuesday, and will be brought to Brunswick, Maine, for funeral services at Brackett's Funeral Home at 29 Federal Street on Friday at 1:00 p.m. The Rev. James Herrick will officiate. Burial will be in the Bailey Island Cemetery.

BRUNSWICK RECORD – May 1965
James C. Shea – OBITUARY

Mr. Shea was born on Bailey Island, November 19, 1920, son of Herbert G. and Hattie Leeman Shea. He attended the Harpswell schools.

A veteran of World War II with service in the Navy, he was awarded a Bronze Star for the Solomon Islands' campaign. He also wore the Victory Medal, American Area Medal, European-African-Middle Eastern Area Medal and an Asiatic-Pacific Amphibious Force Medal.

Since returning to civilian life he was engaged in fishing, serving on sardine boats, seiners and draggers.

He is survived by his widow, Mrs. Marie Deshon Shea, Brunswick; two stepsons, Joseph Peterson and Vincent Oppedisano, both of Brunswick; two sisters, Mrs. Selina Freeman of Bailey Island and Mrs. Ira White of Brunswick; several aunts, uncles, nieces and nephews.

My mother received the following letter in answer to her inquiries regarding the nature of her brother's death:

Office of the County Prosecutor   *June 3, 1965*
Ocean County Court House
Toms River, New Jersey
08753

To:
    Mrs. Selina Freeman
    Bailey Island, Maine
Re: Investigation of death of James C. Shea

Dear Mrs. Freeman:
In answer to your recent inquiry into the referenced matter, this office, in cooperation with the Point Pleasant Police Department, investigated this matter, and through information and investigation, we have determined

this to be an accidental death.

Through investigation, we have determined that on the night of March 11, 1965, around 6:30 PM, James Shea, in the company of several other male companions, was having a party aboard the boat, Fred H Snow, said boat tied up at the company pier, Point Pleasant Beach, New Jersey. Mr. Shea had not been seen since that night, and subsequently reported missing to the Point Pleasant Beach Police Dept., along with his automobile, a 1950 Dodge Coupe.

At 6:51 AM on May 16, 1965 the body of James Shea was recovered from the Manasquan Inlet by the US Coast Guard. An autopsy was performed. Results of the autopsy disclosed submersion as the cause of death, no indication of foul play.

With regard to his automobile, though a stolen car message has been broadcasted on the vehicle, it has not been recovered. It is the understanding of the undersigned that this car was available to any one of the clam-diggers for their use at any time, and is quite possible this car has been abandoned in some out of the way place.

In regard to the alleged threat on Mr. Shea's life, this was alleged by Mr. Shea before he disappeared and could not be substantiated by any of his friends other than what he had told them. The suspects were interrogated in this matter to the degree of a polygraph examination.

Hoping this is the information you desire. If not, please feel free to contact the undersigned at any time.
Very truly yours,

Calvin Woolley
Chief of County Detectives.

23
Selina (Celina) Shea Freeman

Selina's Childhood Memories

"During the first part of my life," Selina wrote, "I remember living just above the Pearl House on Orr's Island. There was a nice lady who lived at the Pearl House, and I remember going to visit her. There was an orchard behind the house, and it was a nice place for children to play."

"My Dad wasn't with us often because he worked as a mason with his father and family in Massachusetts. When he was home he lived with his parents and siblings at Little Island. We visited at Little Island often. Even as small children Eileen and I were very close. Although she was my aunt and my father's baby sister, we were almost the same age.

"When I started school at Orr's Island we walked about one mile to school. I had a big sister, Marie, who was almost five years older than me and my brother, Jim, was two years younger.

"Grampy and Grammy Linscott lived in the old house at Little Island. Grammy was a famous Midwife. They told us she delivered two hundred babies and never lost a baby or a mother. I remember the day she died. Uncle Joe Shea came to tell us, and we were all very sad.

"Without knowing why, we moved to Bailey Island. Grampy Leeman came and got us in a boat and we moved into Clayt and Winona Johnson's house across from the Bailey Island General Store. We were there

Grampy Leeman holding Young Harold, Marie, Selina, Jim & Grammy (Bessie) Leeman

through 1924 and 1925.

"It was during those two summers that I went to Damariscove Island with Grammy and Grampy Leeman. Grampy went lobster fishing from Damariscove. The Coast Guard Station on the Island was in full operation at that time and there were five to eight families living there. Since there were no small children on the Island, I got really spoiled. I loved it, and never forgot what a happy place it was for a child.

"The house we lived in for the summer was known as the White House. Grammy wallpapered the rooms of the house with her old left-over paper she'd brought from home. She didn't care if it matched or not, as long as it was clean.

"A third of the house was used as a school and I spent many hours playing school with my dolls there. The school part of the house was about ten by fourteen. I remember the floors were made with wide boards that had huge cracks. There were eighteen desks and they were all screwed to the floor. The desks had the kind of top that lifts up and there were inkwell holes for inkbottles on one side of the top. The teacher's desk was up front and there were slate blackboards on all four sides of the room.

"The summer I spent at Damariscove Island with Grammy and Grampy, my mother worked at the Green Shop in the Fargo Building. At that time it was an Ice Cream Parlor and Gift Shop on the Steamboat Road. I think Marie helped out some doing dishes and odds and ends

Hattie at Work – Green Shop on the Steamboat Wharf Road – 1926

of things. I really did miss my mother and Marie and Jim. I remember when I came home I hugged my mother's legs and cried.

"Mother always worked hard and was such a dear mother. We were poor but it was a time when you didn't mind being poor. She always gave us a quarter to use for pleasure, if she had it. We would go roller skating or to the movies on Orr's Island. We were never told we couldn't afford it. I'm afraid my dad was a charming, loving man, but he did not contribute to our support.

"We moved into the apartment in my Grandfather Leeman's house when I was eight. Grampy Leeman had an old Brownie and he got it started one day and we all went for a ride. The Island had very narrow dirt roads then and there were no cars and very few horses and wagons.

"The Steamboat coming to the Island four times a day was really interesting. They delivered the mail, coal, food, news-

Jim & Selina Shea, Young Harold Leeman

papers and building materials. It was exciting to see the boat come in to the wharf. More romances started there! People dressed up a lot, especially the summer people. We thought they were all rich.

"The hearse that was used for funerals was always driven by Gramp Murray. It was a glassed-in wagon that was hauled with a horse. Whenever there was a funeral, all of us kids would walk along behind the hearse and cry like we thought we should. Gramp Murray wasn't really my grandfather but acted like a grandfather would. We felt very close to all the older people on the Island and called them Grammy, Grampy or Aunt and Uncle. There was always a lot of love on this little Island!"

Scarlet Fever & the Quilt

It was in the spring of 1930-31 when Marie Shea and Ira White were courting that Marie got scarlet fever and had to be quarantined. Marie and Ira were very much in love, and during the time of her confinement the only contact they had with each other was through their letters and an occasional visit with a closed window between them. The separation was more painful to them than the illness.

Marie was kept apart from the rest of the family, as well. Marie's mother Hattie took care of her in the apartment on the other side of Grampy Leeman's house on Bailey Island. During this time Marie's younger brother and sister, Jim and Selina, were also quarantined and lived in the other half of the house with Grampy (Elisha) and Grammy (Bessie Powell) Leeman.

To keep Selina and Jim busy and out of trouble, Hattie and her mother Bessie came up with the idea of having them make a quilt. With Grammy Leeman's help, they cut out and hand-stitched enough quilt pieces together to make a full-size quilt. They had finished the top section of the quilt when they were finally able to leave the house and go back to school.

My brother Gordon and his wife, Judy, recalled hearing my mother tell the story of the quilt and what a special memory it had been for her. They wondered what had become of it and asked her about it. From what she could remember, it had gone to her sister Marie's house on the Hacker Road in Brunswick. Aunt Rhea had passed away in June of 1986. After her estate was settled her grandson, Dale Perreault, bought the house and was living there. Our mother was quite sure that the quilt could still be there. *(This discussion took place in the 90s.)*

Gordon and Judy talked to me about the quilt and asked if I'd mind going to the house with Dale's mother, Ercil, to see if we could find it. I talked to Ercil, and we made plans to go there and look around. Dale met us at the door and told us to take our time and assured us that everything in the attic was just the way his grandmother had left it. I described the quilt top to Ercil, and she did remember seeing it there years before.

When Ercil and I were little girls we used to play in the attic after the wasps that wintered there had left. We were much younger and smaller the last time we crawled on our hands and knees through the small opening and only entrance to the attic space up under the eaves. Once we got inside and looked around with our flashlights, we could see there were boxes everywhere. Systematically, we started going through the boxes of memorabilia. They were filled with outgrown clothing, unfinished craft projects and patterns, old school and family pictures, children's books, toys, dolls and doll clothes, etc. Aunt Rhea and Uncle Ira White's family history was all stored there. It was a trip down memory lane for both of us.

We had rummaged through most of the boxes and were down to the bottom of the last box of sewing and fabric when we found what looked to be the quilt-top. Anxious to see, we carefully took it out of the clear plastic bag, unfolded it and opened it

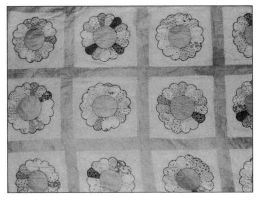

The Scarlet Fever Quilt

up. Sure enough, there it was! After more than sixty years the pink, white and calico patterned quilt-top with all the uneven little stitches was still bright and in one piece.

I was so pleased to have been successful in finding it that I drove to Gordon and Judy's house in Dresden that same day. Since it had been their idea to recover the quilt, Judy kept the quilt top and got the necessary materials to finish it. It was early fall, so there was still plenty of time for her to fill it, sew the backing on and tie it off before Christmas.

You can imagine our mother's surprise when she opened her Christmas gift that year! The gift that opened warm memories of a time of confinement when she was 13 and her little brother Jim was 11 and their Grandmother Leeman taught them how to make a quilt.

Selina meets Phil Freeman

It was Armistice Day, November 11, 1931 and 13-year old Selina Shea was in love! Selina and her 17-year old sister, Marie, had spent the evening dancing at the Library Hall on Bailey Island. Men danced with their wives, mothers and daughters. Beaus danced with their special girls, and small children danced with each other. The old danced with the young and "do-see-doed" the "light on their feet" and the heavy old ladies. In no time the hall was filled with the warmth of all their hot, sweaty bodies.

It was a cool night and a fire had been laid and lit in the rusty cast iron stove that sat in the back corner of the hall. And although the fire had long since died down, the hall got warmer and warmer as the evening went on. Young Selina had danced most of the slow dances with Phil Freeman that evening. Her friends had told her that he was from Brunswick and his father had been the "Insurance-Man" who came down from Brunswick each week to collect insurance premiums from the Island people.

Selina knew that Mr. Freeman had been sick and that the family lived on a farm up in the New Meadows area of Brunswick. Her girlfriend Georgie Smith said, "Phil was a junior at Brunswick High School until

19-year old Phil Freeman   *14-year old Selina Shea*

his father got so sick last year that he had to quit. Phil's been staying at
George and Vidie Johnson's house ever since. They're real good friends
of the family, and they gave Phil a room, and George put him to work
on his lobster smack down at Mackerel Cove."

Georgie knew Selina was sweet on Phil and thought he was much
too old for her friend. She told her, "Phil's been seeing George and
Vidie's niece June York, you know. You want to watch out for him. They
say he's quite the ladies' man. Oh, I know you think he's pretty special
with his big broad shoulders and those soft blue eyes of his. Never mind
that thick shock of blonde-brown hair that he always combs just so with
that flip of a wave in the front!"

Georgie went on and on and couldn't be stopped. "I've heard all
about Phil Freeman! They say he even bedded that neighbor of his in a
hay mow on their farm in Brunswick. Heard he did that before he was
even old enough to shave. Actually, if the truth of the matter be known,
this girl was older than Phil by a few years and she probably seduced
him. But, that's beside the point. Look out for him, that's all!"

All the warnings and well meaning advice from Georgie and her
other friends went in one ear and out the other. Selina was in love. This
handsome young man had spent most of the evening dancing with her.

Of all the other girls at the dance he could have chosen to dance with, he had chosen her.

The magical evening and the last waltz had just ended and the "Musical Johnsons" were packing up their equipment for the night. Lin Johnson had played the "bones" alternately with the drums. His mother, Ethel, was at the piano and his father, Orrin, played the violin.

Selina went in the back room to get her coat and when she came back, she couldn't find her sister. Her friend Dotty Doughty saw her looking and said, "If you're looking for Marie, forget it! She left with Phil Freeman a few minutes ago. I heard Phil ask her if she needed a ride home, and she sure didn't waste any time saying yes." Selina couldn't believe what Dotty was saying. He couldn't have taken Marie home instead of her! Why didn't Marie tell her?

"Come on, Selina," Dotty said, "Walk home with me and Barbara. We'll protect you from the ghosts and goblins going by the cemetery and the three of us should be safe from Old Jim!"

Just as they were leaving the hall, a brand new black Ford sedan pulled up out front. Phil rolled down the window, leaned out and said, "Hey, Selina, want a ride home?"

(Phil drove Marie home and dropped her off, then he came right back to the hall for Selina.)

1931 Autograph Book

December 12, 1931
"To keep my friends, what few I have
Is my delight
So in this book
I pray you'll write."
Nena
Selina Mae Shea

You may fall from the window!

 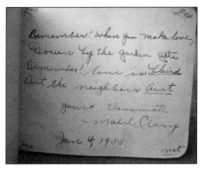

Selina's 1931 Autograph Book

You may fall from above
But for heaven sakes, Selina
Don't fall in "love"
Mabel Clary
("How can she help it.")
its (Dangerous)

Out in the moonlight under a tree, sits two lovers.
Who could it be?
P.F.S.S. Your Schoolmate, Marion

Phil loves Selina, Selina loves Phil
Phil loves carrots, Phil loves squash
Phil loves Selina and he does by gosh.

When you are old, and cannot see
Put on your specs, and think of me.
Jerry

When you are old and washing dishes
Think of me and my best wishes.
Jeannette Johnson

When you are married and have your nine

Feed them ice cream and they will be fine.
Raymond Johnson January 4, 1933
By hook, By crook,
I'll be the last one,
To write in this book.
Your Schoolmate, Lila Baker
January 4, 1933

January 6, 1933
Please don't go down to the wharf before the boat.
SS and PF will be there. P.S. You might hurt your eyes.
Paul

Big Letters—P.F. X S.S.
Down in the freight yard, who did I see, Dotty and me?
P.F. X S.S. in P.F. ARMS

Forget Me Not
Dorothea Geneva Skillings—
Bailey Island Grammar School

Remember me now, Remember me ever
Remember the good times, we've had together.
Always a friend, Dottie (How about the green camp?)
Don't forget the Scout meetings and Mrs. Knorr.
"Ever remember an auto without any lights?"

Roses are red, Violets are blue
Sugar is sweet, but you are SOUR!
John Murray, Jr.

In the parlor, there were three
Selina, the parlor lamp and he.
Three is a crowd, there is no doubt.

So the parlor lamp went out. January 9, 1933
Ernestine Lubee

If you read this book without my consent
You'll have to suffer the consequence.
If this book should chance to roam,
Box its ears and send it home to Miss Selina Shea.

Selina Shay so they say goes to the Whistparty every day.
Inez York—Grade 5 - Bailey Island Grammar School

When you are married, and have your children nine,
Bundle them up and come over and see mine.
Best Wishes,
James Shea
January 10, 1933

January 20, 1933
May your virtue ever shine
Like the dew on a pumpkin vine.
Lila Baker

April 3, 1933
As I was going up the hill
Who should I meet but Nena and Phil
This is what I overheard!
I love you!
Georgie Smith

When you get married and have twins
Don't come to my house for safety pins.
Your loving daughter, Janet Freeman Nov 17, 1947—Age 8—
Bailey Island Primary School

(Mom's Autograph Book must have been out and I decided to write in it too!)
Author's Note: Please disregard punctuation and spelling errors. I transcribed these writings as they were written.

School Picnics at Jaquish Island

During the last years of Mum's life, Land's End at the southernmost tip of Bailey Island was one of her most favorite places to be taken for a drive. With neither of us feeling the need to talk, we'd just sit there in the car and look out towards Jacquish Island. The view always brought her back to her childhood and especially her memories of classmates and the annual end-of-the-year Bailey Island School picnic.

"To this day, I can still see our teacher, Margaret Skillings, and puntloads of fellow classmates and supplies being rowed out to Jaquish Island where we would spend a beautiful sun-filled day in June. We'd come ashore on the beach at Jaquish. Margaret hand carried a canvas bag that held her cast iron frying pan, a few cooking utensils, flour, a jar of egg wash and some grease.

"A green five-gallon army surplus metal can with a good carrying handle held our drinking water for the day. Lots of small bag lunches, a couple of galvanized buckets and a few clam hoes emptied the punts of their cargo. There was not a cooler or picnic basket in sight.

"Most of us kids would start right in picking up driftwood along the shore and in no time had a good size woodpile. While we were getting firewood, Margaret and a couple of the boys would build a small rock fireplace and get a good hot fire going.

"The rest of us kids would start taking turns with the clam hoes. Each one of us would dig a dozen or so clams and then pass the clam hoe on to the next in line. Then we'd take the clams we'd dug, wash them at the water's edge, shell them out and go over to where Margaret had set up quarters on a ledge next to the fire.

"First she'd dip the clams in a little egg wash and then drop them into the flour mixture in her cheesecloth bag. She'd shake the bag gently to coat the clams with a fine layer of egg 'n flour. Then she'd drop them, one at a time, into the hot grease of the old black cast-iron frying pan. Each addition would pop, sputter and spatter as the freshly dug clams hit the hot fat.

"The child who had dug the clams she was frying at the time stood patiently by with his tin plate in hand waiting for the clams to be cooked and ready to eat. This process would go on until each of us kids had eaten the clams we'd dug, cleaned and shelled. I can still see Margaret to this day, sitting there on the ledges, with her dress spread out around her, frying clams for all of us kids."

Mum went on to say, "I honestly believe Margaret Skillings to be one of the best teachers I ever knew. She started teaching when she was only sixteen. You know, all they needed was a certificate to teach in those days. She taught my mother Hattie, me, my sister Marie, my brother Jim and our son Gordon. Three generations!"

Note: The above is a story I recreated from one of the stories she shared with me during her lifetime.

Story of the Doves

My mother's first memory of the doves was at the Old House on Little Island. This was the home of her great-grandparents, Moses and Mary (Mamie) Linscott. Sometime later, the old folks gave the doves to their daughter Julietta and Jeremiah Shea for their new stone house at Little Island. Mum said, "I can still see

them on that shelf over the kitchen stove where they always sat holding pencils, and they were in the same condition then as they are to this day."

She went on to tell me how they came into her possession: "After the death of my father, Herbert Graham Shea in 1959, my brother Jim and his wife, Marie, bought the house at Little Island. Juliette (Sis) Lubee was visiting at Little Island one day while Jim and Marie were cleaning out the house. They were just getting themselves settled in and were busy sorting through things. Several boxes of trash sat there in the kitchen all ready to go to the dump on Great Island later that day.

"Sis glanced over to the box right next to her chair and there sticking out from the very top of the box was something vaguely familiar to her. Sis had spent a lot of time at Little Island during her childhood and she, too, remembered the doves on the shelf above the stove! She asked Marie if she could have them. Marie was happy to oblige and Juliette took them home with her."

Mum went on to say, "Years later Juliette and I had lunch and were spending the afternoon together at my place on the Harpswell By The Sea Road on Great Island. We'd had our lunch and were just getting ready to have coffee when Juliette got up from the table and went over to where she'd left her bag on the rug by the door." She said, "Nena, I have something very special that I want you to have." You can imagine our mother's reaction when she saw the doves that held such warm memories of Little Island and her childhood.

The doves were always treasured by our mother, and although our kids never knew the full story, they knew Nanny Freeman loved doves! Over the years she received many other doves in the form of pins, earrings, stationary, planters, knick-knacks, Christmas ornaments, etc. In fact, a dove is on the stone that marks her final resting place.

After Mum's death in 2002, Gordon and Connie thought that since I had written a story about the doves, I should have them. I kept the doves on a shelf and enjoyed them for quite a few years. Then after spending time and sharing memories with my cousin and dear friend Shirley (Shea) Hudson I told her about the doves and asked her if she remembered them. Shirley had grown up at Little Island, but had lived away from Maine and the Islands for many years. She remembered them well and just as my mother had . . . sitting on the shelf above the kitchen stove holding pencils. She couldn't believe they were still in existence, and I told her the story of how they came to be first in Mum's and then in my possession.

After talking with Gordon and Connie, they agreed and with all our blessings we gave the doves to Shirley, who treasures them for her memories of Little Island as much as our mother did.

How Many Times

A Tribute to Celina Shea Freeman
Written by Deborah Lynn (Baribeau) Achey
And Read by Debbie at her Grandmother's Funeral February 8, 2002

How many times, Nanny, did we stop in for a visit to spend a minute, only to stay for awhile and leave with more than we brought?

How many times did we rush in from our busy lives only to be calmed by your steadfast spirit and gentle heart?

How many secrets did you hold within your heart? Stories, things all of us had shared knowing you would never reveal what was closest and dearest to our hearts—what was preying on our minds?

How many times did you lighten our load—comfort us, encourage us, remind us that these were the "best days of our lives," and truly they were— I believe you now, Nanny.

How many times were you available and willing to just go with the flow, just as long as you had your most prized possessions with you, your dear family?

How many times did you speak about that circle of love, that circle of life— those family ties that bind us to each other forever?

How many times did we pick crabs together? Share a game of Upwords or Scrabble? Share a meal, a recipe? Share a story about you and Grampy, you and your children, you and your travels to Ireland, Germany, and Hawaii?

How many times did we enjoy your accomplishments? The pride you took in receiving that high school diploma at age 58 and then your CNA certificate?

How many times did you answer the phone with such joy, happy to be included in our day, anxious to hear about our lives—always minimizing your struggles, your pain?

How many times were you present at July 4th reunions, eating lobster and clams with everyone, encouraging us to make the rounds and spend time with cousins and other relatives we hadn't seen in a year?

How many times did you welcome the spring in with crocuses, johnny-jump-ups and begonias; digging up that first spring vegetable, dandelion greens? Savoring rhubarb picked fresh from the garden?

How many times did you arrive home to Maine after spending the winter in Florida—just to be here in time for Mayflowers and when you couldn't pick them yourself, others made sure you had them to enjoy?

How many times did you cross that Cribstone Bridge, ride the Island roads, watch the sunsets, and appreciate all that you had for roots on the Island?

Memories of working at Rock Ovens Restaurant, owning and operating Mackerel Cove Market with Grampy, and speaking about days on Little Island?

How many times did we call you Mum, Nanny Freeman, Aunt Nina, Neen, Celina, Sis, and Mama? How many times did we call you our friend?

24
Janet Freeman Meets
Dennis Baribeau

T he Topsham Fair was always held in October, and during the
week of the Fair most schools in the area took Wednesday off
so everyone could go. It was a special time that people of all
ages looked forward to from one year to the next.

In the fall of 1953 Nancy Johnson and I were both sophomores at
Brunswick High School (BHS) and ready for a day of fun at the Topsham Fair. We left home that morning wearing our black wool school
jackets with our names sewn diagonally on one side of the front and
"BRUNSWICK" in big orange letters across the back. We'd washed and
curled our hair the night before, and thought we looked pretty cool in
our new dungarees with the wide folded-up cuff!

Nancy's father Linwood drove us to Topsham and dropped us off on
Elm Street where we paid our admission and walked through the gate
to the Fair. They had a special price for students on Wednesday so, if
we were careful, our money might last us the whole day.

We decided to walk around for awhile to see what they had for new
rides this year and which ones looked like the most fun. After walking
up and down the midway a few times we stopped to watch the
"Hootchy-Cootchie" girls who were outside trying to lure a few men
inside for the next show. There was music playing, and a crowd had
gathered to watch the girls dance on the small stage in front of the tent.
Watching them embarrassed us after awhile, so we walked on and de-

cided to go on a few rides.

The "Tilt-a-Whirl" wasn't new, but it was always fun, so we went on that ride first, and then to unwind from our turning and spinning, we went on the Ferris Wheel. While we were on the Ferris Wheel we could see a long line in front of a new ride called the "Bullet." It was silver and shaped just like a bullet. Even though the kids on the ride were screaming, it seemed to be the most popular ride on the midway.

Nancy and I were standing next to the ticket booth trying to get up enough courage to buy our tickets for the Bullet when a couple of guys started talking with us. We didn't know either of them, but they seemed nice enough so we introduced ourselves and discovered they were BHS students, too. Bill Ormsby was a junior and Dennis Baribeau, a senior.

They were fun to talk with, and in no time the four of us were laughing like old friends. We were still unsure and hesitant about going on the ride, but when they told us they'd pay for our tickets if we'd go on the ride with them, we went!

It was definitely the scariest ride at the Fair that year. In fact, it was probably the scariest ride we'd ever been on. But after our first time around we had so much fun that we went on it over and over again.

When we'd finally had enough, the four of us walked around the fairgrounds together and got to know each other. The guys threw baseballs for awhile and tried to win a stuffed animal. They did all right, but weren't quite good enough to win a prize.

Then to show us which one was the strongest, they took turns with a big mallet trying to hit the disc at the bottom hard enough for it to go all the way up to the top and ring the bell. Anyone who could ring the bell won a prize and the admiration of everyone standing around watching them! Neither of them quite made it, but we all laughed a lot and had a good time.

I thought Dennis was pretty cute! He wasn't very tall but he had a lot of dark brown hair that he combed like "Fonzy" on "Happy Days," and from the very beginning I loved his soft, expressive brown eyes. On the day of the Fair he was wearing a brown leather flight jacket over a green plaid wool shirt, and he and Bill were both wearing dungarees that were folded up and cuffed like ours. We all hung out together for the rest of the day, and Dennis and I hit it off from the start. He was kind of shy, and so was I. At the end of the day when the guys walked us to meet our ride home, Dennis asked me if I'd like to go to the BHS football game with him on Saturday. I said yes.

Three days later we went to the game together, and I have to say this was the beginning of our courtship and falling in love. It wasn't long before Dennis asked me to go steady with him. In the 1950s when you were asked to go steady with someone, the guy would give you his class ring to wear on a chain around your neck. This would show everyone that you were taken.

In those days Bailey and Orr's Island kids who went to BHS had to ride to town on one of the privately owned Ouellette buses. It cost each student $1.50 a week to ride the bus, and it was a long ride to and from the high school every day. We had to make all the stops along the way and go all the way down the Cundy's Harbor Road to pick up the kids there. Most days we'd still get to BHS early enough for Dennis and I to see each other before the first bell.

We'd meet at a little store called the Log Cabin that was close to the high school. There would be just enough time to see each other for a few minutes and exchange the notes we'd written the night before. During the school day we'd try to see each other whenever we got a chance, but there was never much time between classes.

Sometimes I was able to stay in town after school and catch a ride home with my father when he got through work. On those days we'd walk downtown from the high school and go to F.W. Woolworth's for a soda. We'd sit at the counter and were happy just having some time together. Dennis'

Dennis & Janet at Bailey Island – 1953-54

Dennis & Janet in Lisbon, Ct. – 1955 Ford

mother, Louise, had a friend and neighbor, Sally, who worked at Woolworth's. She told Louise, "Those kids are really in love. You should see how they look at each other!"

The school year of 1953-54 was a good one for us. We had fun going out to the movies, football and basketball games or just spending Sunday afternoons together at the Island. There were so many special times we shared that year . . . Christmas, Valentine's Day, Dennis' Senior Prom and his BHS Graduation in June. Dennis picked me up for most of our dates in the Baribeau's family car, a 1941 Hudson, known as the "Tank." If we were lucky, Dennis was able to get his father's 1952 two-ton Dodge dump truck for the movies at the Opera House in Bath on a Sunday afternoon. We thought the truck was great because it had a radio and a heater that actually worked!

Even though we'd been so close and shared so many things that year, I began to think it might be nice to have the freedom to go out with other boys if I chose to. I'd had very little dating experience, and Dennis and I had been seeing each other steadily since before I turned 15.

I did break up with him that summer, returned his class ring, and we both dated other people over the next couple of years. Except for the few times we ran into each other, we didn't see each other for almost two years. When we finally got back together it was like we'd never been apart!

25
Johnson-Leeman

My great-great grandfather, Thomas C. Leeman, was born of Samuel and Caroline W. (Hall) Leeman on December 28, 1835 in Georgetown, Maine. Thomas' first marriage to Sarah J. Wilson on January 22, 1858 ended with her death August 21, 1858.

Thomas then married Alvira Jane Johnson on May 18, 1862. A few months later he enlisted in the Twenty-fifth Maine Regiment on September 29, 1862. He mustered out on July 10, 1863. After Thomas came home from the Civil War he was a fisherman on Bailey Island until his death on June 29, 1895.

Alvira Jane was the daughter of Almira (Sprague) and Captain Elisha Allen Johnson of Bailey Island. Alvira's mother, Almira Sprague, was born at Small Point, Maine on May 11, 1816. She was the daughter of Jethro Sprague of Small Point, who married Nancy Malcolm of Bath. Almira was the seventh generation from the Ancestor Francis Sprague, who came to Plymouth, Mass., on the ship Ann in 1623.

Almira's husband Captain Elisha Allen Johnson and his brother Captain Ephraim Johnson served as captains on a number of fishing schooners including the 55-ton Vine which they owned together. Captain Elisha also captained the Garland, Fairplay and Georgia on their numerous fishing voyages to the Bay of Fundy and other fishing areas.

Alvira Jane Johnson was raised, along with her ten siblings, in the house her grandfather Captain David Johnson had built for his family on Bailey Island. The Johnson's family home was to become home to Thomas and Alvira Jane Leeman after their marriage. It was here that they raised their seven sons and only daughter, Almira May. My great-grandfather Elisha Stephen was the fourth child born to Alvira and Thomas Leeman. Alvira Jane was still living in the same house in 1907.

When I was a young child growing up in this small neighborhood of Leemans and their offspring, the Johnson-Leeman house was occupied by the Herb and Jessie Leeman family. Herb Leeman was a direct descendant of Thomas C. Leeman.

City Of Bath Record of Marriage

Thomas C. Leeman of Bath, Maine, married Sarah J. Wilson of Bath, Maine - January 22, 1858

Book 3 - Page 113

Death Notices of Thomas Leeman's 23-year old brother, William, and his 45-year old father, Samuel, who died within a month of each another:

Eastern Argus Newspaper –

July 16, 1853—In Winnegance, 16th instrument, William H. Leeman, aged 23 years died of disease at home.

August 16, 1853—Mr. Samuel Leeman of Winnegance, aged about 45 years, died off Block Island on board the brig, Monticello, where he worked as a mariner. The Monticello was on her passage from Savannah to this port in Bath, Maine. Mr. Leeman was buried at Holmes Hole at sea. He has left a family at Winnegance.

Thomas was only 17 years old when his brother and father died of disease. At a very early age he went to work running his own saw at the mill in Winnegance. When he was 21 he went to work in a steam sawmill for Scott Morse of Bath. He remained there for several years.

Thomas named his seventh son Scott Morse Leeman.

Thomas' grandfather, Samuel Leeman, was born in Woolwich in 1763 and died in Bristol, Maine in 1833.

Samuel served in the Revolutionary War and was listed in:
Soldiers, Sailors, Patriots of the Revolutionary War
(9299.1S684-1982) Pension #S1893

Union Church at Bailey Island

The early settlers of Harpswell came from Massachusetts, and most were direct descendants of the Pilgrims who had landed there in 1620. There was no church building in Harpswell at that time so services were held in homes and conducted by local men. A preacher known as a "circuit rider" would come to the Island once a year to hold services for the residents. Later, the citizens of Harpswell built a meeting house at Harpswell Center, and the folks from Bailey Island would cross Merriconeag Sound by boat and walk more than a mile to worship at the Chapel there.

Deacon Timothy Bailey bought the Island in 1750 and built his home near the north end of Bailey Island. Tired of the long trek to Harpswell Center, Deacon Bailey and others went back to holding services in their homes. They continued this practice until David Johnson gave them a small building to use for worship and a school.

By 1880 they outgrew the small room, and a group of Bailey Island ladies got together to organize a sewing circle which they called the Willing Helpers. Their goal was to work toward a church building. Twenty men and women joined to sew and put on suppers in their homes.

On May 23, 1880 they had a legal document drawn up, and they became incorporated as the Bailey Island Sewing Circle. The group was organized for social, moral and religious purposes.

The first officers were Lizzie A. Johnson, President, and Sarah A. Sinnett, Vice-President. My great-great-grandmother, Alvira (Johnson) Leeman, served as Secretary until her death on May 8, 1919. Her mother, Almira (Sprague) Johnson, served as Treasurer until her death April 28, 1891.

My great-grandfather, Elisha Leeman was not a church-going man. However, he was very proud of his mother and grandmother who worked so hard to raise money for the building of the church, and who continued to serve actively in the earliest years of the Union Church on Bailey Island.

From donations, fairs, sales, sewing and suppers they eventually raised $1,300. Orr's Island residents even became involved and would row over to Bailey Island to help with fund-raising events and to attend functions. As soon as Captain James Sinnett gave them the land for the church in 1885, they began to build. The cost of the building was $1,350.

Union Church at Bailey Island

Direct Descendants of Jonathan Hatheway Johnson

1. Jonathan Hathaway Johnson b. Abt. 1690 in Sweden
   d. in London, England
   m. Anna Frazier

2. Jacob Johnson b. Abt. 1715 in England
   d. October 15, 1803 in Bailey Island, Maine
   m. December 17, 1752 in Harpswell, Maine - Abigail Bibber
   b. Abt. 1727 – d. April 20, 1813 in Harpswell, Maine

3. Jonathan Johnson b. October 4, 1754 in Harpswell, Maine
   m. 1st Mehetable Hasey
   m. 2nd May 1, 1776 in Harpswell, Maine - Miriam Booker
   b. June 23, 1755 in Harpswell, Maine

4. David Johnson b. December 15, 1780 and d. June 20, 1840 at Bailey Island, Maine
   m. December 24, 1803 in Harpswell, Maine - Abigail Allen
   d. July 2, 1826

5. Elisha Johnson b. June 20, 1817 and d. November 9, 1901 at Bailey Island, Maine
   m. July 13, 1839 at Small Point, Maine – Almira Sprague
   b. May 11, 1816 at Small Point, Maine – d. April 28, 1891 at Bailey Island

6. Alvira J. Johnson b. November 10, 1840 and d. May 8, 1919 at Bailey Island, Maine
   m. May 18, 1862 in Harpswell – Thomas C. Leeman
   b. December 18, 1835 in Georgetown, Maine
   d. June 29, 1895 at Bailey Island, Maine

7. Elisha S. Leeman b. April 18, 1870 and d. 1962 at Bailey Island, Maine
   m. December 5, 1889 in Harpswell - Betsa E. Powell
   b. October 10, 1871 at Cundy's Harbor, Maine
   d. May 23, 1941 at Bailey Island

8. Hattie E. Leeman b. March 28, 1898 and d. July 12, 1952 at Bailey Island, Maine
   m. November 12, 1913 in Harpswell – Herbert G. Shea
   b. January 17, 1896 in Harpswell – d. August 14, 1959 at Bailey Island

9. Celina M. Shea b. April 15, 1918 in Harpswell – d. February 4, 2002 in Brunswick, Maine
   m. October 21, 1933 in Seabrook, New Hampshire – Philip A. Freeman
   b. June 11, 1913 in Lynn, Mass., d. December 3, 1983 in Togus, Maine

10. Janet Freeman b. December 26, 1938 in Brunswick, Maine
    m. July 6, 1957 in Brunswick – Dennis G. Baribeau b. July 8, 1936 in Brunswick

Direct Descendants of Samuel Leeman

1. Samuel Leeman b. 1639 in Boston, Mass.
   m. July 20, 1666 in Boston – Mary Longley
   b. in Charlestown and d. June 21, 1714 in Charlestown, Mass.

2. Nathaniel Leeman b. August 27, 1677 and d. 1735 in Charlestown, Mass.
   m. 1st Abt. 1712 - Thankful Henshaw
   m. 2nd January 5, 1714/15 in Charlestown - Mary Hutchinson
   b. June 21, 1699

3. Samuel Leeman b. March 20, 1725/26
   m. November 22, 1755 in Montsweag, Maine – Abigail Slowman
   b. 1734 in Montsweag – February 2, 1821

4. Samuel Leeman b. April 3, 1764 in Woolwich, Maine
   d. April 30, 1833 in Bristol, Maine
   m. April 3, 1788 in Georgetown, Maine - Jane Hall

5. Samuel Leeman, Jr. b. 1807 in Bristol, Maine
   d. July 30, 1853 - Buried at Sea
   m. November 27, 1828 in Georgetown, Maine – Caroline Hall
   b. December 5, 1806 in Georgetown

6. Thomas C. Leeman b. December 18, 1835 in Georgetown, Maine
   d. June 29, 1895 at Bailey Island, Maine
   m. 1st January 22, 1858 in Bath, Maine – Sarah J. Wilson d. August 21, 1858
   m. 2nd May 18, 1862 in Harpswell, Maine – Alvira J. Johnson
   b. November 10, 1840 and d. May 8, 1919 at Bailey Island

7. Elisha S. Leeman b. April 18, 1870 and d. 1962 at Bailey Island, Maine
   m. December 5, 1889 in Harpswell – Betsa E. Powell
   b. October 10, 1871 at Cundy's Harbor, Maine
   d. May 23, 1941 at Bailey Island, Maine

8. Hattie E. Leeman b. March 28, 1898 and d. July 12, 1952 at Bailey Island, Maine
   m. November 12, 1913 in Harpswell, Maine – Herbert G. Shea
   b. January 17, 1896 in Harpswell – d. August 14, 1959 at Bailey Island

9. Celina M. Shea b. April 15, 1918 in Harpswell – d. Feb. 4, 2002 in Brunswick, Maine
   m. October 21, 1933 in Seabrook, New Hampshire – Philip A. Freeman
   b. June 11, 1913 in Lynn, Mass., d. December 3, 1983 in Togus, Maine

10. Janet Freeman b. December 26, 1938 in Brunswick, Maine
    m. July 6, 1957 in Brunswick – Dennis G. Baribeau b. July 8, 1936 in
    Brunswick, Maine

26
Linscott-Shea

The Linscott Family in Harpswell

Our first Harpswell ancestor was Joseph Linscott, Jr., who was born at York, Maine on February 2, 1723. Joseph married Elizabeth Peakes in York on June 6, 1748. Shortly after their marriage they left York and settled in Harpswell. Joseph and Elizabeth (Peakes) Linscott were listed as pioneer settlers at Harpswell, Maine in 1750. In 1755 Joseph was appointed a Harpswell town official. This was the beginning of a long line of Linscotts in the town of Harpswell.

At that time Harpswell was known as Merriconeag Neck. The land was covered with stately trees, and its woods were full of wild animals. Joseph bought a farm on Great Sebascodegan Island with its coastline of sharp rock cliffs and ledges. There was one rough trail that led from the Island to the village of Brunswick. He built his home on a high point of land on Great Sebascodegan Island, now known as Great Island. Elizabeth, true to her pioneer spirit, created a home that brought peace and joy to all those who entered its door. Many tales of the Linscott's hospitality are still preserved in family stories.

Joseph became a fisherman and was known at sea as one who could not be frightened by any storm or gale. He was considered one of the most adventurous fishermen on the Maine coast and was said to be a man of the truest and grittiest stock. Many of the Linscott's neighbors were from some of the finest families of Massachusetts. They were quick to admit that Joseph Linscott, Jr. was a man of true integrity and a great help in the town of Harpswell.

Joseph's great-granddaughter, Mary (Linscott) Patterson of St. Paul, Minnesota, remembered visiting at Great Island every summer. She said, "I remember the old house near the Orr's Island Bridge on Great Island. My grandfather Samuel Peakes Linscott and his wife Dorcas (Dunning) began their housekeeping there. Old residents of Bath and close relatives of the Linscott family assured me that this place on Great Island was indeed the original Linscott Homestead."

The first of three generations of Linscotts named Moses was born at Great Island in 1758 and died on February 24, 1814. Moses was known as a man of great integrity and strength of character. He married Hannah Wilson, who was the daughter of William Wilson of Harpswell.

The second Moses, Moses Linscott, Jr., was born May 20, 1785, and was known throughout the region as a brave seafaring man. He was lost at sea in 1809. A black stone marker with his name and date of his death can be found in the Cranberry Horn Cemetery on Great Island.

Moses, Jr. and his wife, Mary (Ridley) Linscott had one child, James A. Linscott, who was born in 1808. Several years after Mary's husband's death, she married Joshua Barstow. Stephen Sinnett of Orr's Island adopted young James and trained him in a truly fatherly manner for his life's work as a fisherman. James Linscott eventually became one of the most successful and best known fishermen on the coast of Maine.

The famous Reverend Elijah Kellogg of Harpswell was a great admirer of James Linscott and often spoke of him with great pride. He was known to say, "The Linscotts don't need help very often, but when they do, what one does for such people is a 100% investment."

On one of the bleakest days in the life of the Linscotts the Reverend Kellogg rowed over to Orr's Island from Harpswell Neck. He went from one house to another with the message, "Captain Linscott has had a hard time of it, but he is not whining. Tomorrow a baby is due at his house. It may be a girl we'll be proud of or a boy who will grow into a skipper who will out-sail every last one of you. Wood? Yes. Haul him some big sled-loads of wood. Could they use flour? Yes. That will be handy."

Within a few hours the Linscott home was the scene of great neighborly kindness. The boy who arrived in the midst of all the helpful gifts became one of the brightest captains on the Maine coast. James and Mary (Black) Linscott's son (the third Moses) was born on July 28, 1842. He was my great-great-grandfather, Moses B. Linscott.

1894 Wedding Invitation – Julietta Linscott & Jerry A. Shea

Moses B. Linscott married Mary ("Mamie") York on April 23, 1864. Mamie gave birth to eight children. Two of their children died in infancy and three during an epidemic of diphtheria in the summer of 1877. It was during one of Captain Moses Linscott's extended fishing voyages that three of their children died and had to be buried right away due to the contagious nature of

the disease. Addie, who was not *Julietta Linscott on her Wedding Day* quite seven, died on June 21, 1877. Her little four-year old brother, Frank, died eight days later, and eleven-year old Julia died on July 3, 1877. When Moses returned from his fishing trip, three of his beloved children had been buried on Little Island. Their small white gravestones can be seen in the Orr's Island Cemetery but, to my knowledge, their remains are still on Little Island.

Eight months after these tragic deaths my great-grandmother, Juli-

Front Page – August 4, 1929 – Three Survivors of Famous Island Family and Their Homes

etta Linscott, was born on March 22, 1878. She and her brother, Moses B. Linscott, Jr., who was born in October 1887 were the only two children to grow into adulthood. Moses, Jr. lived to be 31. Another brother, Fred, died in 1901 at nine years and ten months. Julietta was the only child born to Moses and Mamie who lived long enough to marry and have a family. She was 80 years old when she died on July 12, 1958.

Jeremiah Augustus Shea and Julietta Linscott were married on September 26, 1894 and had nine children including one child who died at birth. My grandfather, Herbert Graham Shea, was their first-born.

Footnote: John Black – born c. 1790 at Orr's Island, died February 6, 1849 Mary Goodrow (or Goodhue) – born c. 1792 at Orr's Island, died

February 9, 1840
John and Mary were married in 1814 and had nine children.
John Black lived at the old house on Little Island and it was known as John
Black's place.
Charles Black, their third child, was born May 11, 1818 at Orr's Island.
Source: Vital Records of Harpswell, Maine

Moses and Mamie Linscott

Captain Moses B. Linscott had three fish stores that were centers for trade on Orr's Island in the late 1800s. They were located on Little Island in Lowell's Cove. Fishermen unloaded their catches and bartered for bait, rope and other supplies there on the wharf with Captain Moses Linscott.

Linscott Home & Fish Stores on Little Island, Orr's Island c. 1912

Moses and his brothers James A., John, William Henry, Isaac and Charles had a fishing fleet of as many as 13 schooners, and Lowell's Cove was the hive of their flourishing industry. At one time the Linscott brothers were the leading characters in the Casco Bay fishing business. They employed over 100 men in their fleet and followed every branch of the off-shore fishing industry.

In the spring they went Salt fishing at the Grand Banks and fished for Browns and LaHave at the Seal Island Grounds. During the summer they fished for swordfish on Georges, and they went trawling during the winter.

Their fishing crews came from Portland, Gloucester, Nova Scotia and the Casco Bay Islands. These men were afforded lucrative employment from one season to the next for a number of years. The Linscotts were known to be lucky fishermen and fishermen up and down the New

England Coast looked for a chance to ship with the Linscotts.

Captain Moses B. became the keystone of the rugged Linscott arch after the death of his father, James Linscott, Sr. in 1866. His brothers said, "Moses could easily have had a bank account running into six figures if his head had ruled instead of his heart. He literally gave away several fortunes and would tell you to this day, he never regretted it one iota."

Orr's Island residents all told the same story about him. Moses' customers came from everywhere to do business at his large grocery and ship stores on Little Island. They loaded what they wanted into their boats and kept their own accounts. Captain Moses even helped load a quarter of beef, along with a full cargo of other supplies, aboard a customer's dory knowing full well he'd never get paid. The good customer always came back though with promises and appeals and went away with yet another load. When friends and relatives questioned his easy ways, Moses replied, "A hundred years from now, I'll never miss a penny of it."

The Linscotts made a lot of money during their long career in the fishing business. William Henry said, "We started out with little or nothing. But, after we bought the Constitution (which proved to be successful) we continued to add one vessel after another. Each one was built new and each one was a financial bonanza."

Linscott Brothers Fishing Vessels

Constitution, Pinky Louisa, Little Dreadnaught, George E Hagen, Willie and Alice, Moses B, Josie Mae, Julietta, Cora E Smith, Mary Smith, Eva and Mildred, Maid of the Mist and others.

When the Linscott fleet was setting its sails and weighing anchor in Lowell's Cove at Orr's Island,

Fishing Schooner – The Moses B. Linscott built 1880

prosperity was at its zenith and fewer ports gave forth an atmosphere of greater commercial activity.

Brunswick Record – February 8, 1923 – Orr's Island News

Mrs. Moses Linscott and Mrs. Adeline Huff are both on the sick list. The Ladies Aid Society of the Methodist Church presented both Mrs. Linscott and Mrs. Huff with a dozen fine oranges and a dozen pinks.

Moses B. Linscott at the Helm

Brunswick Record—June 7, 1923

In the passing of Mrs. Moses B. Linscott our Island has lost one of its most respected residents. Mrs. Linscott was a woman of most amiable disposition, kindly in all ways to those with whom she came in contact. The latch-string to her home always hung on the outside of her door, and her ministrations to those not as well blessed with this world's goods gave evidence of her hospitality and generousness. She will be sadly missed by those suffering from sickness or poverty as she was always ready for calls from either class at all hours of the day or night. No person ever passed from her door hungry or lacking words of comfort if in distress.

Mrs. Moses B. Linscott (Mary aka "Mamie") was a midwife for many years on the Islands. She could be seen traveling by boat or walking along the Island paths and carriage roads carrying her little black bag to tend to the sick or deliver a new baby. I was told she delivered over 200 babies during her lifetime and never lost a mother or a child. She

Mary "Mamie" (York) & Moses B. Linscott at home.

delivered all of her daughter Juliette and Jeremiah Shea's nine children. The original birth records list Mary (York) Linscott as the Attending Physician, and her signature graces their birth records as well as the records of many other Island families.

Note: *Mamie smoked a pipe and in her older years was sometimes referred to as, "Dirty Mamie."*

Brunswick Record—Captain Moses B. Linscott

Linscott Homestead at Lowell's Cove on Little Island c. 1910

The funeral of Captain Moses B. Linscott was held at Orr's Island on Thursday, June 19, 1930. Captain Linscott was in his 88th year and of that good old New England stock famous for their hospitality. Captain Linscott was a life long resident of Orr's Island.

Captain Linscott at one time owned and was master of his own fishing vessel which bore his name.

Captain Linscott is survived by his daughter, Mrs. Jere Shea, with whom he has made his home since the death of his wife six years ago. He also leaves a number of grandchildren.

Shea Family Story

John Shea and his 26-year old son, Michael, worked as gardeners on the Downey estate in County Cork, Ireland. The Downey's lovely 16-year old daughter, Bridget, was attracted to Michael and followed him around the grounds whenever he was there. After a time, her parents became aware of their mutual attraction and demanded that she stay away from the hired hand.

They still managed to see each other, fell in love and hoped to get married. When Bridget found herself pregnant a month after her seventeenth birthday, she went to her parents to tell them of her condition. She knew in her heart that now they would have to accept her love for Michael. She was wrong. The Downeys vehemently withheld their blessings and forbid the marriage.

(I have no record of a marriage in Ireland at the time of this writing, but assume that one did take place in County Cork in c. 1853-54. A son, John Andrew Shea, was born to Bridget and Michael in Ireland, March 25, 1854.)

Bridget and Michael left Cork County, Ireland from Queenstown (Cobh) and arrived in the United States in June 1854. My guess is that the young couple decided to leave their newborn son with Bridget's parents until he was older, stronger and better able to withstand the hardships of a lengthy ocean. According to my research, John Andrew Shea didn't leave Ireland until he was 17 years old. He left County Cork from Cobh (now Queenstown) and arrived in Boston September 27, 1871.

Family members in Ellsworth have told us that Bridget and Michael crossed the Atlantic on a very crude boat called a cattle boat. We were told they landed in Pinking, Nova Scotia and walked down through Calais, Maine with a man named Laffin. They stopped at lumber mills along the way for food and shelter. Eventually they arrived in Ellsworth.

In those days Ellsworth was a bustling town of 3,000 residents. In 1852, for example, five ships, brigs or schooners were built in Ellsworth. It was said that on one day in May more than sixty vessels were tied up at the wharves there.

When they first got to Ellsworth, Michael did mill work and the couple lived in a boardinghouse on Turner's Hill. Later he worked as a stone mason, and they moved into a two-story house on Grant Street. In those early days Grant Street was known as Paddy Lane, since so many Irish lived there. I was told many of the houses were built with lumber found floating down the Union River.

Aunt Jere (Jeraldine Shea) Mowat said, "I remember visiting Grammy and Grampy Shea at their house on Grant Street in Ellsworth. The one thing that stands out in my mind is the stairway that led to the second floor. I remember going upstairs and at eye level, on the wall next to each stair, was a different religious picture." Since Aunt Jere shared this memory with me, I've wondered if the pictures could have been depicting the "Way of the Cross."

Bridget and Michael supposedly had 13 children. However, I have only found records of eleven. It's very possible there were two more births that resulted in early deaths.

A son, Michael A. Shea was born in Ellsworth on October 22, 1856 and married Minnie A. Brown. Michael and Minnie always lived in Ellsworth. He was the barber in town, and although he was known to be a poacher, he was also the local game warden. They had seven children, and many of the seven remained single. This family was said to be psychic. People said they communicated with the dead, used the Ouija Board, made card tables rise from the floor, and other psychic phenomena.

Another son, Patrick Henry Shea was born May 3, 1858 in Ellsworth. He was a custom tailor and had his own shop in Ellsworth. I was told he had a bad leg and always walked with a cane. Patrick married Sarah "Sadie" B. Bragdon in 1889, and they had three children.

The Sheas practiced the Catholic faith in Ireland, but Catholicism was relatively new to New England in the mid-1800s. During that time the Jesuits were setting up missions all over Maine, and the Catholics of Ellsworth had acquired a building to use for a church. In 1853 Father Bapst, a Jesuit priest, set up his residence in Ellsworth, Maine. He and his parishioners worked hard to build a new Catholic Church that was finished just in time for Christmas Mass in 1853.

In June of 1854 Father Bapst was forced to leave Ellsworth due to problems he was having with the Protestants. He returned late on Saturday night, October 14, 1854, planning to say Mass the next morning for his old parishioners. When word got out that he was in town a mob gathered, entered the house where he was a guest and carried him away. They took his watch and wallet, stripped him, plastered him with hot tar, daubed with feathers, posted and jostled him on a rough plank and left him unconscious. These men, who were thought to be of such noble character, had almost killed Father Bapst, and destroyed the old and the new Catholic Church.

This was the atmosphere in Ellsworth, Maine when Bridget and Michael Shea arrived there in 1854. It was a time when the inflammatory Know-Nothing Party and its anti-immigrant platform were popular, in part brought on by a flood of immigrants fleeing the famine in Ireland. The local populace feared for their jobs and for the burden the new immigrants were putting on welfare services, schools, hospitals and the like. The Know Nothing Party declined after the 1856 elections.

Jeremiah A. Shea's House at Little Island - 1910 Lowell's Cove, Orr's Island, Maine (Note: Picture was taken from the back of the house.)

Stone House on Orr's Island

Stone House

While summering on Orr's Island, Varney had admired Jere Shea's house on Little Island. "a rugged house of native stone" built c. 1910 by Shea on Little Island. He built this house after his previous house on Rt. 24 burned to the ground.

Varney spent 12 years collecting field stone for his Stone House on Orr's Island. Construction took two years.

The Stone House was built by Orr's Island mason, Jere Shea, c. 1924 for Justin Varney.

"Shea, assisted by James W. Thurston did all the masonry. Charles Thomas, assisted by Lendall Stilphen and Arthur Danforth, did a credible job on the interior woodwork and cabinetry.

"The mahogany used with such effectiveness in the parlor and the den came from the Bay State National Bank in Lawrence, Mass., where Varney served as president for many years. The bank had been remodeled and modernized shortly before the Stone House was started. Mr. and Mrs. Albert Ouellette took possession of the house after Mr. Varney died. This building also housed a gift shop at one time that was also called The Stone House. The gift shop was relocated to Bailey Island in 1980."

Note: The above quotation was taken from a Brunswick Record article written by Margaret Todd c.1949.

Source: Historic Preservation Survey U-33-45, dated 12-5-1980, Cumberland County, Harpswell Little Island Road, Orr's Island and U-32-38 dated 10-14-1980

Jerry Shea's Stonework-Seymour's Chimney – Orr's Island

Brunswick Record –
Orr's Island News –
June 14, 1923

Dr. Nash of Lewiston has rented the Shea Bungalow at Little Island and with his family will occupy it for the season. The Shea bungalow is

Jere Shea and his brothers worked on the Union Station in Portland, Maine. The granite terminal was razed in 1961.

Julietta & Jeremiah Shea

one of the best on the island and in a very sightly location.

Brunswick Record – July 6, 1934
JEREMIAH AUGUSTUS SHEA – OBITUARY

Residents of Orr's Island regret the passing of a beloved and respected member of the community, Jeremiah Shea, who died suddenly at his home of heart trouble.

Mr. Shea lived on the Island for many years. He was an excellent mason and noted for his rustic fireplaces. He was also prominent in politics.

Funeral services were held at his late home, and conducted by Rev. Frank Welch, pastor of the Methodist church. Mr. Shea is survived by his wife, Julietta (Linscott) Shea and also Mrs. Lawrence Allen of Lexington, Mass., Mrs. Richard Dickson, Mrs. Walter Leeman of Saugus, Mass., Miss Geraldine Shea of Lexington, Mass., Harold Shea, Herbert Shea, Joseph Shea, Miss Eileen Shea and several grandchildren. Interment was at the Orr's Island cemetery.

Direct Descendants of John Linscott

1. John Linscott b. August 5, 1655 in Exeter, St. Peter Cathedral, Devonshire, England
   d. December 27, 1711 in York, Maine
   m. 1st Between September 1, 1689-1690 in York, Maine – Lydia Milbury
   m. 2nd 1696 in York, Maine – Sarah (Kingsbury) Brookings

2. Joseph Linscott b. 1695 in York, Maine
   m. Between 1719-1720 in York, Maine – Hannah Bragdon

3. Joseph Linscott, Jr. b. February 2, 1723/24 in York, Maine
   d. January 11, 1787 in Harpswell, Maine
   m. June 6, 1748 in York, Maine – Elizabeth Peakes
   b. August 12, 1712 in York, Maine

4. Moses Linscott b. 1758 at Great Island, Maine
   d. February 24, 1814 at New Meadows, Brunswick, Maine
   m. Abt. 1784 in Harpswell, Maine - Hannah Wilson

5. Moses Linscott, Jr. b. May 20, 1785 at Great Island, Maine
   d. Abt. 1809 – Lost at Sea
   m. May 5, 1808 in Harpswell, Maine - Mary Ridley
   b. November 14, 1788 at Great Island - d. April 8, 1840 in Harpswell

6. James A. Linscott b. 1808 at Orr's Island, Maine – d. October 12, 1866 in Harpswell, Maine
   m. 1st Harriet Webber August 9, 1832 – d. Abt. 1834 in Harpswell
   m. 2nd March 15, 1838 in Harpswell - Lucinda Black
   b. October 1, 1820 and d. September 10, 1839 at Orr's Island, Maine
   m. 3rd 1840 in Harpswell – Mary Black b. 1816 – d. Sept. 16, 1889 at Orr's Island

7. Moses B. Linscott b. July 28, 1842 - d. June 17, 1930 in Harpswell, Maine
   m. April 23, 1864 in Harpswell - Mary M. York
   b. July 1, 1848 and d. May 23, 1923 at Orr's Island, Maine

8. Julietta Linscott b. March 22, 1878 and d. July 12, 1958 at Orr's Island, Maine
   m. September 26, 1894 at Orr's Island - Jeremiah A. Shea
   b. March 21, 1872 in Ellsworth, Maine - d. July 6, 1934 at Orr's Island

9. Herbert G. Shea b. January 17, 1896 in Harpswell - d. August 14, 1959 at Bailey Island, Maine
   m. November 12, 1913 in Harpswell, Maine – Hattie E. Leeman
   b. March 28, 1898 in Harpswell – d. July 12, 1952

10. Celina M.. Shea b. April 15, 1918 in Harpswell – d. Feb. 4, 2002 in Brunswick, Maine
    m. October 21, 1933 in Seabrook, New Hampshire – Philip A. Freeman
    b. June 11, 1913 in Lynn, Mass., d. December 3, 1983 in Togus, Maine

11. Janet Freeman b. December 26, 1938 in Brunswick, Maine
    m. July 6, 1957 in Brunswick – Dennis G. Baribeau b. July 8, 1936

Direct Descendants of John Shea

1. John Shea b. in County Cork, Ireland
    m. in County Cork, Ireland - Ellen Sliney

2. Michael Shea b. September 21, 1827 in County Cork, Ireland
    d. December 22, 1912 in Ellsworth, Maine
    m. About 1853 in County Cork, Ireland - Bridget F. Downey
    b. May 1836 in County Cork, Ireland
    d. November 5, 1882 in Ellsworth, Maine

3. Jeremiah Augustine Shea b. March 21, 1872 in Ellsworth, Maine
    d. July 6, 1934 at Orr's Island, Maine
    m. September 26, 1894 at Orr's Island, Maine – Julietta Linscott
    b. March 22, 1878 at Orr's Island, Maine
    d, July 12, 1958 in Harpswell, Maine

4. Herbert Graham Shea b. January 17, 1896 in Harpswell, Maine
    d. August 14, 1959 at Bailey Island, Maine
    m. November 12, 1913 in Harpswell, Maine – Hattie E. Leeman

5. Celina Mae Shea b. April 15, 1918 in Harpswell, Maine
    d. February 4, 2002 in Brunswick, Maine
    m. October 21, 1933 in Seabrook, New Hampshire – Philip Albert
    Freeman
    b. June 11, 1913 in Lynn, Mass., - d. December 3, 1983 in Togus,
    Maine

6. Janet Freeman b. December 26, 1938 in Brunswick, Maine
    m. July 6, 1957 in Brunswick, Maine – Dennis George Baribeau
    b, July 8, 1936 in Brunswick, Maine

27
Lawrence Elwell Johnson

Several years after my father's death, my mother married Lawrence Johnson. He was her uncle by marriage before he became her husband. After he and my mother were married Larry shared stories of his youth and athletic years with us.

Lawrence Elwell Johnson was the second child and only son of Mary Isabel (Black) and Walter Elwell Johnson. He was born on August 19, 1909 at Bailey Island, Maine. Larry had one sister, Marjorie, who was a teacher in the Portland schools for many years. After her mother's death, she ran the Willow Cottage on Bailey Island.

Larry's father died when Larry was 15 years old. After her husband's death, Aunt Isabel (as she was known to most folks on the Island) turned her home into a boarding house for summer visitors. She provided rooms, small cottages and full dining facilities at the Willow Cottage.

Aunt Isabel's accommodations at the Willow Cottage were so favorable that her varied line of guests came back from one year to the next. Since Larry was the only boy and always a big rugged guy, he was called upon to do all sorts of different chores. When there weren't enough rooms to accommodate a heavy guest list he even had to give up his room and bed for a few nights. Larry said, "I didn't mind really. It only happened a few times when it got real busy."

Over the years Aunt Isabel worked at updating her facilities. The one thing her guests complained about most was using the outhouse. One winter when she was making plans for the upcoming season, she had one of her handymen put together "make-shift" bathroom commodes for each of her guest's rooms. The holding tanks for the commodes had to be emptied quite often. Of all the different jobs Larry did over the summer, this was the one he dreaded the most! First, he had to fill a bucket from one of the holding tanks and then carry it away (a bucketful at a time) to dump in the alders down back; repeating this process until all of the holding tanks were empty.

Once in awhile some of Aunt Isabel's special guests would request "Maine Steamed Clams" for dinner. Getting the clams was another one of Larry's chores. If you were an early-riser, you might see Larry leave the Willow Cottage pushing a wheelbarrow at dawn. He'd be headed up the road to catch the early morning tide at Water Cove. After a few hours of strenuous digging he'd be more than ready to start the long walk home. He said, "You know, my feet were dragging as I pushed that wheelbarrow full of clams up Dr. McCarty's hill, and I thought to myself, I certainly do hope those folks appreciate their evening meal tonight!"

Larry definitely earned his keep during those busy summer months at the Willow Cottage. He told us, "I was pretty handy around the kitchen, too, but more than likely they'd have me peeling canning kettles full of potatoes and vegetables or they'd put me in the dishpan to wash those endless piles of pots and pans after everyone had eaten and left!"

I remember when Larry first came into our family, and we had invited him and my mother over for a turkey dinner. I always cooked the neck and giblets with celery and onion to make gravy. Dennis had sliced the turkey breasts and carved a lot of the dark meat as well. After we were all seated at the dinner table, Larry looked at the platter of turkey, and then asked if we had the neck and giblets. He said, "You know, when I was a kid and my mother was running the Willow Cottage the choice cuts of meat, poultry, and seafood were always reserved for the guests! So, I guess after awhile I got so I favored the less desirable parts of the bird. I do like the wings, but the neck and giblets have always been my favorite!"

Brunswick Record—1951

Willow Cottages—Dining Room Opened:

Kitchen: Mrs. Perley Sinnett, Mrs. Linwood Johnson, Mrs. Alfred Smith, Mrs. Royston Leeman

Dining Room: Pam Leeman, Sue McMackin, Yvonne Sylvester

Marjorie Johnson, Proprietress

Larry's Athletic Years 1925—1935

The following pages are written as Larry spoke them in 1993.

"I remember it all starting about 1924," said Larry. "I used to follow my cousin, Rip Black, around. Rip, five years older, was my idol. I wanted to be just like him. He was a world-class hammer thrower and football player. Rip went on to win the Bronze for the hammer throw in the 1928 Olympics in Amsterdam.

Larry (center) with friends next to his car.

"I'd go with Rip to the field out back of the Library Hall on Bailey Island. I'd watch him practice, retrieve the hammers for him and try throwing a few of my own. I think you might still be able to find a hammer or two that got left behind in those days of practice back in the 1920's.

"I entered Portland High School in 1925. Up to that time I had never seen a football game, never mind play in one. I signed up for the team my first year and that proved to be a learning experience. I was slow, but enthusiastic from the very beginning. In my second year I made

Portland High Weight Star Believed Real Prospect For A National Title

Larry Johnson

Larry Johnson – Portland High School Weight Star

the first team and played fullback. I was also chosen as fullback that year for the All-Maine team. The following year, which was my third year at Portland High School, once again I was chosen as fullback for the All- Maine team, but also for the All-New England team.

"I remember well the game that ended my football career. It was the last game of the season, and we were playing Deering High on a frozen field. I slipped on my knee on the frozen ground and tore cartilage. I had to have cartilage removed and other re-pair work. The injury resulted in one leg being shorter than the other. That injury also led to back problems later. The doctor said this would be the end of my participation in any future athletics. Being stubborn and encouraged by a good friend and football trainer, I massaged and exercised my knee.

"Although the injury did end my football career, I was able to continue in track. I started track in my first year of high school and won every event in hammer throwing and most of the discus and shot-put events. My second year I won all three events during our high school schedule and in the statewide track meet. That year I was also presented with a cup for Athlete of the Year. My fourth year I also won all three events in track.

"My knee had improved enough that year for them to send me to Chicago where I won third place in a National Discus competition. Due to a lack of competitors, the hammer throwing event was discontinued in Chicago that year.

"In 1929-1930 I went to Maine Central Institute (MCI), a preparatory school, in Pittsfield, Maine. I won all events in hammer throwing, discus and second or third place in shot-put. I was known as the MCI Boy. An insurance man stated, 'If MCI can train an athlete that well,

TRACK TEAM

ack Row: C. Lucey, R. Craven, M. Bernstein, F. Kimball, E. Iverson, Coach R. Corey, R. Jone
N. Doherty, C. Kahill, D. Boone.
ird Row: J. Meehan, C. Peters, S. Hider, C. Moody, M. Karlin, R. Dunbar, E. Gardner, P. Conro
W. Silverman, R. Hanson
cond Row: Asst. Mgr. O'Rourke, Mgr. E. Resnick, W. Daly, R. Rosenberg, Capt. L. Johnson,
Kelsey, J. Dolan, R. Poland, Asst. Mgr. F. Schreiber.
rst Row: J. Elowitch, Dzio-Dzio, S. Brenerman, E. McKeough, H. Siewertsen, M. Cragin, K. Kop
lowitz, N. Coe, A. Pacillo

Track Team – Portland High School Yearbook – 1929 – Larry 2nd Row, Center

I'll donate funds for a new athletic building.' I do remember there were pictures of me on display in that building.

"At Brown University and Prep School I won the New England Track Meet. In hammer throwing I threw almost 200 feet, and they said it was a National Prep School record, about 30 feet beyond the former mark. At the New England Track Meet I was offered an athletic scholarship by Track Coach Ted Merideth from the University of Pennsylvania. It included tuition, room, board and spending money. I readily accepted! I spent my freshman year there. Shortly after that, they had a good housecleaning and abolished all athletic scholarships.

"My sophomore year I transferred to Bates College in Lewiston. I was still on a scholarship, but worked in the kitchen and did other jobs as needed.

Larry getting his trap gear ready for the season.

"In the spring of 1932, trials were held in Cambridge, Mass. to see who would qualify for the Olympics being held in Los Angeles that July. My cousin Edmund F. (Rip) Black and I both competed in the hammer throwing event. I won first place with a heave of 169 feet 6-1/2 inches and Rip qualified with a throw of 160 feet 6-1/2 inches.

"Two Bailey Island boys, who were cousins, had qualified for the pre-trials of the 1932 Olympics! There was only one cloud on the horizon; during the trial competition I had strained my back once again.

"Rip and I crossed country by train with other Olympic teammates going to the Olympics in California. I was favored to win the medal in the Hammer Throwing competition. But, due to the problem I was having with my back I couldn't practice as I should have and was not able to stay in the circle. I did throw one of my best throws ever, but it didn't count. There was a question about the coach calling it a foul, but who knows…?

"I never did much traveling, but Rip and I did travel to athletic meets in Pittsburgh, Pa. all expenses paid. We'd order steaks that were so big they'd overlap the 18-inch platters they were served on!

"I did attend another meet in Chicago where I received an honorary medal for athletic achievements. I was recruited for Annapolis, but would have had to serve a hitch in the Navy and due to a punctured eardrum would not have passed the physical. I also worked for awhile in a training camp as a riding and athletic instructor for aged and over-weight businessmen. The doctor at the camp offered me a scholarship for the University of Illinois, all expenses paid. I also had other offers in this country and outside of this country to participate in athletic events, but I had to refuse them all due to family responsibilities back home on Bailey Island."

28
Edmund "Rip" Black

E dmund "Rip" Black of Bailey Island was a high school star in four sports at Portland High School (PHS). Besides playing baseball and hockey, he was named Maine's best high school fullback in 1923 and became the captain of the PHS track team.

He entered the University of Maine at Orono and began to garner national attention as a hammer thrower. He graduated to the 16-pound hammer and in 1928 won the Olympic trials in the event at Harvard University Stadium in Cambridge, Mass. This secured him a spot on the Holland-bound SS Roosevelt to enter the Summer Olympics in Amsterdam. Rip was going into his senior year that fall. Rip said later, "In my junior year at UMO, I felt strong enough to beat anyone in the world."

On the day of the Olympic competition, Rip's warm-up throws were traveling more than 175 feet. His competition throw, however, landed well short of his expectations. He said, "I got nervous, tightened up and threw 160 feet 10 1/2 inches to win the Bronze. The event was won by Patrick O'Callaghan of Ireland, who threw the hammer 168 feet, 7 inches."

In 1929 Rip beat the winner of the Gold in the British Empire Meet in London. His best throw ever was 180 feet!

Olympics–1928–Amsterdam

1. Patrick O'Callaghan	IRL	168ft—7in
2. Ossian Skold	SWE	168ft—3in
3. Edmund Black	USA	160ft—10in

Reference: The Complete Book of the Olympics–1992 Edition–Little Brown–Wallechinsky, Track and Field–pages 115-116

Hammer Throw

The hammer is a 16-pound metal sphere attached to a grip by means of a string steel wire not longer than 3 feet, 11 3/4 inches. This potentially dangerous sport appears to have had its origins in the practice of sledge-hammer throwing in fifteenth and sixteenth century England and Scotland.

29
Phil Baker

P hil Baker was 81 years old on May 1, 2003. If I'd been on Bailey Island that day, I would have hung a "May Basket" on him. When I was growing up we lived down the hill from Phil and Bea, and we always got a kick out of hanging a basket on Phil for his "May Day" birthday. Every year I think of him when May 1st comes around.

Phil lived on Bailey Island all his life and was still running a "gang" of 600 lobster traps until his sudden death in August 2005. When I visited him a few years before he died, he spoke fondly of his boyhood friend, Gus Johnson, and the pranks they used to pull. Chuckling, he told of the time he and Gus waited until services had begun at the Union Church down the road and then pouring buckets of boiling water on the pigs in the pen. They thought it was great fun just to make them squeal while everyone was in church!

He went on to tell the story of hand digging a well for Phil's Uncle Clayt Johnson when he and Gus were just kids. Clayt lived at that same house until his death. His granddaughter, Jackie, lives there today. Phil said, "To my knowledge they're still using the same well and still drawing good water from it! We went down 17 feet and got paid 25 cents an hour." Phil went on to say, "You've got to remember, every bit of dirt that was dug out of that well, had to be brought back up in a 10-quart bucket!" He guessed that Uncle Clayt must have had just about the cheapest well ever dug on Bailey Island.

"Speaking of wells," Phil Baker added, "Bish Orr used to line wells with rocks, you know. . . He'd climb down into the well, and whoever was up above would lower a bucket filled with rocks down to him. Bish would choose the right size rocks and chink them in. Well, this one day, Bish was down in the well, and Young Gus Johnson and I were sorting the rocks to send down. One of the rocks we'd meant to toss aside went down into the well! We stood there a minute waiting. Nothing! Then we both stepped over to the edge and looked down into the well. There was Bish looking up at us. He had his hat in his hand and was rubbing his head. He hadn't said a thing!" Phil said, "I guess I forgot to mention, Bish never was a man to waste his words."

Phil had some more stories to tell me about Bish. He was quiet for a few minutes, and after giving it some thought he started in. "Did you know that Bish's real name was Sinnett Winfield Orr? No, well it is, and did you know that Bish Orr was one of the best net-menders around? There isn't an Island fishermen around who would beg to differ on that one. Bish had his own technique, and it worked! He used a wooden match instead of a needle. . . the way his mother had taught him years before.

"Although Bish lined wells and was a master at mending herring nets he spent most of his life as a fisherman. When he was just a young man, he went all up and down the Atlantic seaboard from the Grand Banks to South America."

Phil said, "I remember hearing a story about Bish being out on a fishing trip one time. It was a bitter cold winter night when out of nowhere a sudden storm came up. Well, 50 year-old Bish lost his balance and fell overboard. It just so happened that his namesake was a member of the crew that night. Bish knew for sure his luck was with him when the special young man didn't hesitate to jump overboard and rescue him from the icy Atlantic waters.

"Bish was always a fisherman. Even in his later years he still fished 60 lobster traps. He'd row his punt out to where his traps were set and haul them in by hand.

"Everyone loved Bish Orr! The year his little house at the head of Mackerel Cove burned to the ground, the Island men all got together and built him a nice little house in the exact same spot. He could still look out and see the house where his grandfather had been born."

Update on Phil

I ran into Phil Baker at Land's End a few years back. He was just leaving the parking area as I was entering. We pulled our vehicles up alongside each other and both rolled our windows down. Right off Phil said, "Did you know Bea died last night?" I knew she'd been sick but hadn't heard, and I was saddened over the loss of a dear old friend and especially for Phil's loss.

Instead of staying in that sad place, we started talking about old times and the good times we'd all shared over the years. We remembered when we had all lived in the same neighborhood, and we even reminisced back to the years when Phil and Bea were first married after he got home from serving in the Navy in WWII. They lived in the apartment in the other side of Grampy Leeman's house until they moved into the house they built next door to Grampy's. Phil and Bea were always very much a part of our family.

I asked Phil if he remembered when our daughter Debbie used to have a beer with him when she was about two years old! He laughed just thinking about it. Dennis and I lived in my parent's house on the Island for a short time when I was pregnant with Lori. Bea would come to visit me for coffee some mornings, and I used to walk up with Deb to visit with her.

Quite often Phil would come in after hauling his lobster traps just when we were getting ready to leave. He had a habit of having a glass of warm beer when he first got in and would pour a little bit in a small jelly glass for Deb. She loved this special time she shared with Phil Baker. It got so he'd no sooner be through the door that she'd open the cupboard door under the sink where he kept his beer. We both laughed at this memory of so long ago.

Then Phil chuckled, and the twinkle was back in his eyes when he said, "I'll never forget the good times and all the laughs we had when we'd get together to play cards and have a few drinks. And remember that Christmas Eve when Bea and I walked down to your house for a little "Christmas Cheer" and your father must have mixed Bea's drinks a little too strong. When we got home that night Bea couldn't for the life of her remember where she'd hid all those gifts she'd bought and wrapped for the kids!"

Phil went on to say, "And how about that time your mother filled your grandmother's electric roaster chock full of baked stuffed lobsters? It doesn't get any better than that!" On that note, we started our vehicles and went our separate ways. For a short time that day we had shared stories that put both of us in a happier place.

30
Alfred Perry

I went to a funeral today and took a trip back over the years to my roots. I saw and thought about a lot of special people who have touched my life and the lives of my family in one way or another. It was October 31, 1993, and I was sitting in the back row of the Family Room at Brackett's Funeral Home in Brunswick with my mother on one side and Larry Johnson on the other. Al Perry was laid out in the front looking quite proper and dignified with his shock of white hair and glasses. I sat there watching the people come into the room. They were all there to honor Al and to offer their sympathies to his family.

The Perry kids were our fourth cousins and our closest neighbors when we were growing up. Reggie was the oldest of the three boys. Then there was Al who was a year older than me and Jackie who was a little younger. A short path led from our house to theirs, and we took that path passing through their yard to go anywhere in the neighborhood.

Pam Johnson, who always lived in our neighborhood and was our fourth cousin, came in and sat down. Pam was my brother Gordon's age and her husband Earle had been in a fatal accident on his way to work a few years before. Bea and Phil Baker came in with their youngest son Barry and his wife Sue. Barry had been undergoing cancer treatments for some time now.

And there was Grace Leeman, my mother's dear old friend, who was just recovering from a triple by-pass. Right behind Grace was Linda

Lawson Baker, the girl my brother Wayne was always in love with. She came in with her husband, Skip Baker, who was on duty that foggy night in May 1975 when the Rescue Unit was called for Wayne's terrible car accident. My brother Wayne was 30 years old when he died instantly after hitting a telephone pole head-on at the intersection of the Pinkham Point Road and Route 24 on Great Island. Skip had grown up with Wayne and got sick when he arrived and saw his old friend.

Nancy Johnson's younger brother Ralph (who always makes me think of Nancy and our friendship) came in with his wife Shari. I'd seen Shari right after our youngest daughter Denice's first baby was stillborn. I'll always remember her compassion. She really understood because their first child had also been stillborn. Alfred Johnson and his wife Priscilla came in, and after signing the guest book and offering their sympathies to Ruth found a place to sit in the other room. Al and Priscilla had also suffered the loss of a son who died far too young.

And there in the front row of the Family Room sat Ruth. She was Al's wife and the mother of their eight children. During those tough times there never seemed to be enough room or money for their big family. But Ruth managed to be a good wife and mother and "made do" with what little she had. It was no secret that Al was an active alcoholic for years. If he were sitting here with us today, he'd be the first one to tell you that.

There were people from all walks of life at Brackett's Funeral Home that day. All the rooms were filled with people who at one time or another had suffered their own personal losses. Where else could one go in today's world where you would know so much about the people you'd see at a gathering such as this?

Al was the third generation of his family to dig graves at the Bailey Island Cemetery. He and his father Arnold and his grandfather Jim Perry had dug the graves of most of the Island folks' loved ones. My mother told me that tears were running down Al's face as he was shoveling the dirt out of the hole for the grave of my brother Wayne. When Mum tried to pay him for his services that day he refused to take any money. Wiping the tears from his dirt-smeared cheeks he said, "I remember when we all used to tease Wayne because he was the littlest kid out in the field. You know, we all played and grew up together in that neighborhood."

With the exception of a short time in 1959-60, I haven't lived on Bailey Island since the spring of 1955. I've lived in-state and out-of-state, in many different homes and in many different towns. I have yet to feel that special bond of caring and fellowship that comes from growing up in a small Island community. Where else could you walk through a cemetery and just about everyone buried there brings back a memory or is one of your ancestors, relatives or a friend?

Mr. Herrick, who was close to 90, took his place at the pulpit in the front of the room, doing once again what he had done so well all his life. Jim Herrick had preached in the Island churches and had officiated at the weddings, baptisms and funerals of most of the families in the town of Harpswell.

From our earliest years our lives revolved around our small Island and the people who lived there. Local events were important and everyone attended because that was our life. As we got older we went to school with the kids from Orr's Island. We got to know them and thought of them as our friends, too, but it's still Bailey Island and the people there that tug at my heart.

It was during my father's long hospitalization in 1952 that Al Perry was especially helpful to my mother. He cut and carried wood, shoveled snow and carried water from up in the field. Anytime anyone got stuck in the snow in the winter or in the muddy ruts in the spring, Al would come to their rescue. He was always a good neighbor and friend.

These were my thoughts and feelings at his funeral service on October 31, 1993. Al was 56 when he died at the Maine Medical Center in Portland, Maine after a brief illness.

31
KKK on Orr's and Bailey Islands

I n the early 1920s Eugene Farnsworth of the Ku Klux Klan (KKK) colonized the State of Maine from his headquarters in Portland. With an enrollment of no fewer than 2,700 members, the KKK eventually claimed control of 14,000 out of 23,000 votes.

About this time the steamboat was making runs from Portland to Bailey Island four times a day. With such a close association between Portland and the Islands it didn't take long to recruit a large number of good Island men to the Klan. In a very short time they came to firmly believe in the principles of Klankraft:

"Service for Humanity, Home, Country and God"

Charlie York, a long-time resident of Bailey Island, sums it up well: "The Ku Klux Klan come to our town in 1924, and I joined. I never enjoyed any Lodge so much as I did the Klan at first. It had the principle of brotherly love for 'feller' members, and there was a high moral tone to it.

"I remember a time the attention of Klansmen was called to the conduct of a man with a wife and children who was chasin' after another woman. The Klan voted that a cross should be burned near his home or on his property, and a committee would be named to put on full regalia and burn the cross. The guilty man could then ask somebody he knew who belonged to the order what was the meanin' of it. He would be told and would be invited to join, which was usually done. As part of the initiation at his first meetin' he was charged with what he done, he would confess, and then go to a central altar with the man he had done wrong to, and ask forgiveness, which was given. The order straightened out a number of messes.

"Biggest time we ever had was Fourth of July, 1925. About a hundred Klansmen, most of 'em from Orr's and Bailey's, had a parade in full regalia at ten o'clock in the morning. They was ice cream booths, cold drinks and 'sandridges.'

"I was in charge of one booth where you could buy three baseballs for a nickel and try to hit an image of the Pope at the back of the tent. A 600-pound tuna and a large shark was hung up for display. We had a grand clam and lobster bake at 6:00 and fireworks after dark."

For awhile the men of the Islands were proud of their membership in this secret society. Feelings began to change when the dues they had to send to national headquarters seemed way too high and the Klan started telling them how they should vote in the presidential election that year. Suspicions were aroused, and they were beginning to think that maybe the Klan might be some sort of a racket. Many of the men came to feel ashamed of their association with the Klan, and when they were approached really didn't want to talk about it.

Charlie York said, "The Klan come to Maine sudden, and I think it done a lot of good. And then it left all of a sudden."

Reference: Charlie York—Maine Coast Fisherman by Harold Clifford

Alberta Poole writes of life in Coming of Age on Damariscove Island 1910-1922: "There was no church on the Island! Charlie York, who was a Methodist and led prayers each evening at the Primrose cottage where he lived, was the closest thing to a church on Damariscove Island. Anti-Catholicism and Anti-Semitism were very pronounced at this time! On this island, as well as the islands of Harpswell!"

The following excerpts from the Brunswick Record newspaper describe the coming of the KKK to the Maine Coast in the 1920's and how successful the organization was in recruiting new members.

Brunswick Record Excerpts – KKK in HARPSWELL
October 30, 1924

There was a very large attendance at the meeting of the Klan last Friday night from all parts of the town, Harpswell and Great Island being especially well represented.

November 13, 1924

A large number of Klansmen from all parts of the town were on the island last Friday night and enjoyed a clam supper and naturalization of several aliens.

Weather permitting, there will be a meeting of the Orr's Island Klan at Cundy's Harbor Thursday night November 13, 1924. Speakers from Portland will enunciate the principles and purposes of the Ku Klux Klan.

November 20, 1924

There will be a meeting of the Ladies Auxiliary to the Klan at Red Men's Hall, Friday evening, November 21. Dr. Lannin, from Portland will deliver an address on the plans and purposes of the Klan. The public have been cordially invited to be present. Dr. Lannin is a very eloquent clergyman and those who may be present will be highly entertained. At the close of the address a supper will be served by the ladies.

November 27, 1924

A large gathering from all parts of the town assembled at Red Men's Hall last Friday evening and listened to an able address given by Rev. Dr. Lannin of Portland on the principles and purposes of the Ku Klux Klan. After the lecture more than two hundred and fifty people partook of a very generous supper, consisting of clam stew, cake, doughnuts and coffee, furnished by the ladies of the Klan.

Several applications for admittance to the Klan were filed. Dr. Lannin proclaimed the fact that there were more than twelve million Klansmen in America and that more than eighty thousand preachers of the gospel were affiliated with the order.

May 7, 1925

There was a large gathering of Klansmen at Red Men's Hall last Friday night from all parts of the town who listened to an instructive and eloquent address given by one of the national Klan leaders from Atlanta, Ga. A fine banquet was given after the lecture and those attending went to their homes more than satisfied with the doings of the evening.

May 21, 1925

A large number of Klansmen from Bath gave a minstrel show and dance at Red Men's Hall last Tuesday night and a large attendance by residents and visiting Klansmen enjoyed the exercises to their full. A bountiful supper was passed out to visitors and others in attendance.

Note: Phil Baker said, "The KKK used to meet in a fish-house at Garrison Point on the north end of Bailey Island. The fish-house was directly across from the Rock Ovens, right where Pirate's Cove Restaurant used to be."

The Ugly Head of the KU Klux Klan
by Philip Curran

My mother and father met when he was assigned to the Orr's Island run on the steamer from Portland. They were married in Brunswick on October 29, 1922. After their marriage they returned to live with her parents in the big house on the shore of Lowell's Cove.

Early in their marriage they moved to one of the two houses on Little Island, which is separated from Orr's Island by only a few yards of water and a short bridge. The only other folks who lived there were the family of owners, Jeremiah and Julietta Shea. Coincidentally, my father and Jere Shea were two of only a few Catholics in the town of Harpswell.

In a field on a hill across Lowell's Cove from Little Island, between the Methodist Church and Red Men's Hall on Orr's Island, the Ku Klux Klan burned a fiery cross in a hateful and bigoted ritual that was then becoming a common pastime in Maine. Although the light from the burning cross could be seen far and wide, it was quite clear who was intended to be frightened and humiliated. The burning cross was intended for our family.

My father told me more than once that he knew who was in the KKK gang. He said he had met one of them face-to-face and laid it on the line to him, although he didn't tell me the names of the others. He apparently lived in forced harmony with the Klan for many years, but he never forgot the incident or who took part in it. He was known throughout Casco Bay as a friendly and tolerant person, but he hated the Ku Klux Klan and all it stood for until the day he died.

Jere Shea stood up to the Klan in his own way, advising them that he would shoot any one of them who ventured across the bridge to his island.

Governor Percival Baxter had said in 1922 that he had observed the growth of the Invisible Empire in other states and that he could not believe that "level-headed citizens of Maine . . . will allow themselves to be influenced by such an organization . . . for men to mask and robe themselves and gather by night moving about mysteriously as though possessed by hidden power resembles the mockery of the Middle Ages. No good can come out of such methods and decent citizens will shun them."

Nevertheless, by 1925 when this event took place, as many as 150,000 Mainers had been signed up in the Klan, and even good Governor Baxter had to admit that it was a very politically powerful intrusion. One of its inherent objectives was "to preserve the United States as a Protestant Christian Nation."

They needn't have worried about my father. As far as I know, he never went into a Catholic church after he married my mother, much to the dismay of some of his sisters. Those were the only terms on which my grandfather would give his daughter up. My father paid the price and didn't look back. Although he was never very faithful or enthusiastic about it, he did take part in the activities of the Methodist Church in spite of the earlier passion of a large number of its members for the Klan.

Note: Phil Curran sent me the above story because it pertained to my great grandfather Jeremiah Shea. I have included it here with Phil's permission.

Johnson's Point on Orr's Island. Photo by Adams Studio, Inc. of Portland, Maine

32

Joanne Johnson Lund

My cousin, Randy Lund, gave me a copy of his stepmother's memoir. I have taken information from "Joanne Johnson Lund's Memories" to write the following story of this extraordinary woman who overcame her handicap and achieved all that she set out to achieve!

Joanne Johnson was born in the back room of the South Harpswell Post Office on April 4, 1916. Old-timers, who could still remember the unusual circumstances of Joanne's birth, loved to tease her about it. She was known locally as the "Parcel Post Baby." When they were first married Joanne's parents, Fred and Emma Johnson, lived in a house that also served as the local Post Office in South Harpswell, Maine. Emma, unmindful that her time to deliver their first child was so close at hand, was in the back room of the Post Office when she went into the final stages of her labor.

Shortly after Joanne was born, they moved to Bailey Island to live with Fred's grandmother, Joanna (Thompson) Sinnett. Captain Henry Sinnett made an agreement with Fred and Emma. The family homestead and all of his estate would go to them, if they looked after his wife and their aging grandmother until her death. He wanted to be assured of his wife's care after his death.

On March 22, 1918, Stanley F. Johnson was born. Joanne's new little brother soon became her idol and role model. Even though he was two years behind her in age, she would follow his lead for most of their lives.

Joanne and Stanley's father, Fred Fairfield Johnson, was born on November 20, 1889. He played baseball for the Boston Braves before he got married and was known as "Homerun Fred." Emma Stover was a schoolteacher from South Harpswell and during their courtship she made it clear to Fred that she would not marry a baseball player. Fred's love for Emma was stronger than his love for baseball, so he gave up his dream of a professional career to marry Emma on December 20, 1914.

During WWI there was a terrible epidemic of flu going around. Joanne got it and became very sick. She developed a high fever that lasted so long that it paralyzed the auditory nerves going from her ear to her brain. It left Joanne totally deaf. It was some time before they realized her behavior problems were due to her not being able to hear. At first they thought she wasn't minding her mother, and her father would punish her for her disobedience.

After they found out she was deaf her mother and grandmother worked with her, teaching her to read lips and to form words, so she could communicate and go to school. She did try a private lip reading teacher three or four times, but it wasn't successful. Joanne said, "The teacher had her own way of doing it, and she couldn't teach me. I had my own way, and that's how it's been ever since."

Emma was left a widow when 29-year old Fred drowned in 1919. Stanley was 13 months old and Joanne was 3 years.

Brunswick Record - May 9, 1919 - Fred Freeman Johnson

One of the saddest accidents occurred Wednesday morning, April 30th when Fred Freeman Johnson of Bailey Island was drowned by the overturning of his power boat, "Zip". The craft was off the extreme end of Peak's Island. Scott M. Leeman and Fred Johnson had the boat loaded with herring and were on their way to Portland to sell them. The Government Minelayer 147, which was sent out in response to Fort McKinley found Scott Leeman clinging to the bottom of the boat in a half conscious condition. Scott said, "They could find no trace of Fred Johnson, who was a powerful swimmer. Scott said the last time he could remember seeing Fred, he looked exhausted and was hanging onto an empty gasoline can. He must have clung to the can for as long as he could, then let go and was drowned."

Mr. Johnson was 29 years old. He married Miss Emma Stover of South Harpswell on December 20, 1914. Surviving are his wife, Emma, a daughter, Joanne and a one year old son, Stanley.

He also leaves his mother and father, George B. and Laura Etta (Sinnett) Johnson and three brothers, H. Elroy, Jesse M. and Philip Johnson all of Bailey Island. He also left two sisters, Leona (Johnson) Stover and Miss Genevieve Johnson and his grandmother, Mrs. Henry Sinnett of Bailey Island. The deceased was held in high esteem and had a host of friends.

Author's Note: Scott M. Leeman was the brother of my great-grandfather Elisha S. Leeman.

Joanne said she was named for her great-grandmother, Joanna (Thompson) Sinnett. She was proud to bear the same name that appears on the boulder at the head of Giant Stairs along with that of her great-grandfather, Captain William Henry Sinnett. The plaque commemorated the gift of a strip of land which her great-grandparents had conveyed to the Town of Harpswell for public use. It was a gift given to the Town to allow any person access to the shore and the Giant Stairs without trespassing on private property. Because of the foresight of the Sinnett family we all have the freedom to enjoy the majestic beauty of the waves rolling up against the rocks on the southeastern, ocean side of Bailey Island where Joanne Johnson used to play.

Joanne's uncle, Elroy Johnson, posed for the Maine Lobsterman Statue sculpted for the 1939 World's Fair. There are now three. . . one at Land's End on Bailey Island; another at the Canal Bank Plaza in Portland; and one on Maine Avenue in Washington, D.C.

Elroy became a well-known figure and made many public appearances because he was the model for the Maine Lobsterman statue. He was also known for his work and his voice in town and legislative affairs that had anything to do with the fishing industry. In her memoirs Joanne speaks of the similarity of her Uncle Elroy to Will Rogers. They were brought together because there was such a strong resemblance between the two men.

Will Rogers even came to Maine and visited with Joanne's grandfather and Uncle Elroy once. Because they looked so much alike, a stage production for the two men was planned. They were to appear on stage and mimic something funny. Unfortunately, Will Rogers died before the scheduled show, and it never came about.

Joanne and Stanley were both marathon swimmers. They would swim five miles out to Halfway Rock from Bailey Island and have lunch with the lighthouse keeper there. After eating their lunch and waiting the required hour after, they'd leave for the long swim back home. This was usually during tuna fishing season, so they'd start swimming home about the same time the fleet was due to come in from tuna fishing. If they got tired while they were swimming they'd thumb a ride back to the Island with one of the fishermen. They prided themselves on *always* swimming the five miles out to the lighthouse, although they cheated a little by usually getting a ride home.

Joanne and Stanley's Uncle Elroy brought home a baby seal for them every summer. He made a pen for their little pet, and at first they'd keep the seal in the pen a good part of the time. After the seal got used to them, they could let him out and swim with him. They'd grab onto his tail and the seal would pull them all through the water.

One morning on his walk down to the shore, Uncle Elroy stopped by where Joanne and Stanley were playing on the ledges and told them not to let the seal out of its pen for an hour because he was going to Portland in his boat. They played around until they thought enough time had passed, but they were getting anxious to let the seal out and go swimming. Stanley and Joanne then went to the screen door in the kitchen and asked Aunt Sadie if it had been an hour since Uncle Elroy left the house. She looked at the clock and said an hour had passed and they could let the seal out.

As soon as they opened the gate to the pen, that seal was gone! They were sure this was the last they'd ever see of him and he'd be lost forever. One hour later the pet seal arrived in Portland Harbor, swimming up alongside of Elroy's boat. Elroy thought the seal, with its keen sense of hearing, could probably hear the motor of his boat all through the water.

Joanne used to go out with the tuna fishing fleet when she was just a young girl. It was her job to "chum" bait. She had to cut up bait for the tuna using big butcher knives and a big chopping block. She'd chop up the bait and throw it in the water around the boat. This was done to attract the tuna and draw them closer to the boat. If anything grabbed onto the bait, it meant they were going to get the hook. And if they took the hook, Stanley would never let it go!

Joanne said, "I'll never forget the time my cousin, Ronnie, took me up in his plane! After we'd been airborne awhile, I looked over at him and noticed he was crying. I couldn't imagine what had happened that would make him cry like that." I said, "Ronnie, what is wrong?" He looked at me and with tears running down his face said, 'You can hear, Joanne!' It wasn't until then that I realized I had been laughing, joking and answering his questions without even looking at him. I could hear! It was amazing! Then we were both crying.

If the change in elevation and atmosphere was just right, it would relieve the pressure on the nerves from my ear to my brain, and I could hear. But, when I came back down, I would be deaf again. After this happened, I flew whenever I could."

When Joanne was 14 her mother remarried, and they moved to Brunswick. Stanley and Joanne were then better able to take part in all the sports at the high school. Joanne followed her brother Stanley in most high school sports. He participated in lots of school activities, and she did the same. They were both marathon swimmers on the Brunswick High School (BHS) swim teams. She also joined the track team and played basketball. She loved sports and followed the different sports teams all her life.

Despite Joanne's handicap, she went on to graduate from BHS, Westbrook Junior College and the University of Maine. After college she took an additional three years of correspondence courses in bookkeeping and accounting. Then she went to work in the New England Ship Yard office doing bookkeeping, typing and payroll.

Joanne said, "Stanley graduated from the University of Maine and went to Westbrook Junior College. He took flying lessons and got his private pilot's license. A short time after that I took lessons and got my license, too." She said, "I made it hard for everyone because whatever he did, I did, or wished I could! When Stanley went into the service, I tried to get into the service, too, but nobody would take me because of my deafness.

"The war years came around, and since I had my private pilot's license I got on the coast patrol. It was an early version of the Civil Air Patrol. One of my missions was to fly classified messages to Newfoundland. I did this for three years and felt I was contributing something to the war effort. It was the next best thing to joining the military."

In later years Joanne worked at a reweaving company and went on to study reweaving cloth in Portland, Maine. She became a master at mending and was known as the "invisible weaver." At first she did mending and reweaving for dry cleaners in the area and then started her own business: "Joanne's Reweaving" in her home on Congress Street in Portland.

Joanne married Austin G. Lund three years after the death of his wife, Beatrice Ella (Leeman) Lund, to cancer. When Austin married Joanne he had twelve children . . . seven girls and five boys. His five sons were all mentally challenged and four of them resided at the Pineland Center in Pownal, Maine. One son, Elwood, worked as a dishwasher in a restaurant in Portland and lived at home with Joanne and Austin. He was very good at his job and worked at the same restaurant until he retired. Joanne and Austin enjoyed having him with them, and it worked out well for everyone.

Author's Note: Beatrice was my grandmother Hattie (Leeman) Shea's first cousin. My grandmother said, "I went to Portland after each new baby was born to help Beatrice with the children and the house. We grew up together and were always very close."

References: The Life Story of Joanne Lund
As told to Teresa O. Prince May 12, 1993 (HRD-661
Portland Press Herald –Obituary - November 14, 1960

Joanne's Favorite Fish Story

Most of the Johnsons went tuna fishing in the summer. Stanley loved to go tuna fishing by himself, and he didn't have a fancy boat. He'd go out in his dory with a hand line.

One day when he was out fishing, he got a good bite. He hollered out, "I got one!" to Uncle Elroy who was always nearby. He had him all right, and the fish was pulling him away from the fleet and out of the bay. The fish was so strong he had to just let him run and get good and tired.

When the fish finally wore out and Stanley got ready to head for home, he was nine miles out. It was 11:00 that night before he came into the cove with his prize fish.

The family had been beside themselves with worry and watching. They breathed a sigh of relief when they heard him whistling as he came up the path to the house. He was quite a sight and his hands were raw.

In his dory, with a hand line, Stanley had caught the largest tuna of the year. His fish weighed in at over 900 pounds and earned him one full year at the University of Maine.

33
Prince's Store at Orr's Island

On the wedding day of Fidelia Sinnett and Sylvanus Prince, January 22, 1854, a small child referred to Fidelia as a real "Princess of Maine." Years later the story shown in quotation marks below was written by Rudolph A. Qualley for the Lewiston Journal . . . *"I remember one Sunday in the old church which is still perched in the middle of Orr's Island. I had done some careless thing during the week and had been sharply reprimanded by my uncle's housekeeper. She told the neighbors to not let their children play with me until I'd been made to feel my shame.*

As I went into the church on Sunday morning, not one of the children spoke to me. They shrank into whispering knots as if I were tainted with some terrible sin. I sat down alone in the old family pew and sadly missed the three girls who usually sat there with me. I was trying to hold back the tears that smarted under my eyelashes when I saw Mrs. Fidelia Prince whisper to her little girl. In an instant she bounded down the aisle and cuddled close to me, slipping three-fourths of her candy heart into my hand. Then I remembered the title given to her mother on her wedding day, 'A Real Princess of Maine!' Yes!"

When Sylvanus was 21 years old he left Brunswick and went to Orr's Island where he started a grocery store on land now known as Prince's Point. Later on he added fish buying to his grocery business. In this way he became interested in fishing-vessel property, and he built large wharves and houses for the curing of fish. He very successfully continued in this business for 48 years.

After retiring from this great life-work he became interested in real estate. He was largely instrumental in founding and building the Methodist Church on Orr's Island where he and his wife were members. For more than 15 years he was superintendent of the Sabbath School as well as a faithful steward and class leader at the School. He and his wife gave largely to charitable causes, and they gave in such a quiet way that none but the recipients knew of their generous gifts.

Sylvanus and Fidelia's youngest daughter, Jennie M. Prince, had a very successful business selling her uniquely crafted souvenirs at the store on Prince's Point. She was especially talented in her hand-painted scenes of Orr's Island on china. These souvenirs were highly prized by the thousands of people who came to that part of the Maine coast.

In 1954 their son, Sanford Jack Prince said, "The general store was founded in 1854 by my father, Sylvanus Cushing Prince and his business partner, Sanford Jack. In its day, S.J. PRINCE and SON was a name known and respected throughout New England. Besides its salt fish, the store handled fishing gear, coal, wood and groceries.

"I learned the secret of processing fish from my father. Over the years the company wholesaled millions of pounds of salt fish to the foreign and domestic trade. I've seen 110,000 pounds of cod and haddock brought here in a day, and it was nothing to handle 50,000 to 60,000 pounds daily. But the salt fish business has gone to the devil," Sanford said. "Prices got so cussed high, I got out of it five or six years ago," he added.

In 1954 at age 92 Sanford Jack Prince, Sr., was still behind the counter and was at the store every day from 7 a.m. to 5 p.m. He was known to say, "All I ever wanted was a fair profit, and my motto has always been: BE HONEST and SQUARE. You know, that motto has helped me all my life."

Sanford J. Prince, Sr., and his wife and life's companion, Harriet E. (Stilphen), raised six children and celebrated over 70 years of marriage. Sanford Sr. spoke fondly of his wife Harriet when he said, "She's a smart girl, a smart woman, and she's a good worker. She was always one to stay home and tend to her own business."

A son, Jack Prince, Jr., joined the firm in 1924 and Prince Sr. turned over the active management to him in 1942. Jack's son, Lowell, worked in Portland where he managed the "Downeaster" plant that processed frozen lobster products. Lowell helped out at the family's store on Orr's Island when he had the time.

Sylvanus Cushing Prince was born March 7, 1832 at Brunswick, Maine, and died February 9, 1908 at Orr's Island. Fidelia was born April 17, 1836 of George Sinnett and Deborah Folsom (Orr) on Orr's Island. Fidelia was the fourth generation from the ancestor, Michael Sinnett, who settled on this Island at a very early date.

34
Mysterious Sinking of the Don
June 29, 1941

I
t was a clear, sunny Sunday morning at Dyer's Cove in East Harp-swell, Maine when the group of 34 men and women boarded the 44-foot Don for a day cruise and picnic to Monhegan Island. Twenty-eight of the passengers were merchants, clerks, shopkeepers, bankers and papermakers from the Rumford area.

Nineteen-year old Norman Foster who had recently graduated from Edward Little High School was hired by Captain Paul Johnson to help with the cruise. Norman was joined by his fiancee, Ramola Brundage, who was visiting from Reparessa, California. The three remaining passengers were Oscar Bridgham along with his daughter, Carolyn Miller, and her husband, Dr. Oscar Miller. They were all visiting their cottage at Dyer's Cove. The Miller's were celebrating their 2nd wedding anniversary. They were all good friends of Captain Johnson who would be at the helm and in charge of the cruise.

Some sources say the cruise was scheduled to depart from Dyer's Cove at 7:00 a.m. and others say 9:00 a.m. Regardless, the Don didn't leave until 9:30 due to the late arrival of several passengers. Paul Thurston, president of the Rumford Falls Trust Company, had been scheduled to take the cruise with his son, but had cancelled his reservations the week before because of the early departure.

The crew put aboard clams and milk for a clam chowder to be cooked and served on the boat. Captain Johnson planned to prepare his famous clam chowder for his guests. With the late start, they planned to get to Monhegan about noon, where they would have a picnic on the shore. They'd leave from Monhegan about 3:30 in the afternoon, getting them back to Dyer's Cove about 7:00 that night.

Joseph Bernier, a partner of Capt. Paul Johnson, was involved in another boat excursion that morning. He was taking a group of shoe-workers out on a fishing trip. He left Dyer's Cove immediately after the Don and followed the cruiser out of the cove. He changed his course when the Don veered off towards Monhegan. Later, Bernier spoke of how calm it was on the water that day and remarked on the only fog he found was a slight haziness on the horizon. That afternoon he returned to Dyer's Cove earlier than scheduled because a big thunder storm was brewing.

Shortly after leaving Dyer's Cove, Capt. Johnson realized they didn't have all the necessary ingredients for the chowder. He decided to stop at Alton Reed's Store at West Point to buy potatoes and onions. The captain and a few of the passengers went ashore and were back on the boat in about a half-hour. As they were pulling out from the dock, Mr. Reed and several of the fishermen agreed that the boat looked top-heavy and overloaded.

When they rounded Small Point at about 11:00 a.m. the lighthouse keeper on Sequin Island said the upper deck was lined with passengers. The Don passed south of Sequin at 11:20 a.m. and disappeared into the gathering fog. This was to be the last definite sighting of the Don on that fateful day.

The Captain was at the helm, which was mounted on the cabin roof. Thirteen of the passengers, mostly ladies, were out on the observation deck. Seventeen men and three ladies were probably inside the cabin. Would it be safe to assume that the Don was pitching with the mild sea that was running in the waters off Small Point and Sequin Island that day? Or, is it possible that one of the ladies on the upper deck saw a porpoise or some other marine life and was excitedly pointing it out to the others? If the ladies had all rushed to one side of the boat, it could have easily rolled over. Most agreed that improper distribution of the passengers could definitely cause the boat to turn over. However, if the boat tipped and turned over, wouldn't there have been something to grasp and hang onto and wouldn't someone have survived?

Harpswell fishermen were familiar with the Don. They said it was a 13-year old Jonesport model and had been built in Nova Scotia. They knew it well in the days of prohibition, when it was used as a rumrunner. It had been built for speed with two powerful Liberty motors, an open cockpit and a high bow.

In 1936 the twin engines were converted into a single, 6-cylinder engine, and an enclosed cabin and observatory deck was added for sightseeing. Fishermen said it was too narrow in the beam. It was not more than 10 feet, when it should have been 14 to 16 feet across. They considered the Don dangerously top-heavy, "even at her moorings."

Lewiston Evening Journal Headlines on Monday, June 30, 1941

Thirty-Five Members of Rumford Party Missing on Cruise from Harpswell to Monhegan

Unreported Since Sailing Yesterday – Fog Slows Search US Weather Bureau in Portland reported severe thunderstorms through the section where the cruise was centered.

A severe electrical storm did take place on the afternoon of the sailing, which was followed by a heavy fog. From the time of the disappearance of the Don until most of the recovered bodies were found, it was a "blue dungeon of fog" in and around Casco Bay.

Paul Thurston, who had cancelled his reservations for the cruise, drove to Dyer's Cove on Monday morning after four of his employees failed to show up for work. Eleven familiar cars still sat there in the grass at Dyer's Cove waiting for their drivers to return. When Thurston heard of the disappearance of the Don he immediately made plans to charter a plane and cover the area himself.

The fog didn't lift on Monday and was thicker than "pea soup" all day. Friends and family arrived at Dyer's Cove from Rumford to wait for news of their loved ones. Coast Guard crews and local fishermen searched blindly for the missing boat and its passengers with no success. Governor Sewall's office ordered Inland Fisheries and Forestry Department planes to be dispatched as soon as possible. Those on shore could hear, but could not see the planes above due to the fog.

On Tuesday morning, July 1st, Claude Johnson found the first body. He had gone out to haul his lobster traps and was a mile and a half southwest of Bailey Island when he saw something bobbing in the water about 50 feet away. At first he couldn't tell what it was, but swung his boat around and saw it was a body. He brought it back to Mackerel Cove at Bailey's Island. This was about 6:00 in the morning. By 1:00 that afternoon, seven bodies had been recovered.

Captain Paul Johnson was found wearing only his shoes and underwear. He had a rope tied around his waist that was attached to a small wooden keg to keep him afloat. Several of the recovered victims were wearing watches that stopped between 11:40 and 11:45. I believe the accident took place Sunday morning, shortly before noon, at some point off Small Point.

The week-long search brought relatives, friends and curiosity seekers to the Harpswell area as well as people just wanting to help. During this time eating establishments in the area offered a one-pound lobster with bread and butter to make a sandwich for 35 cents or a crabmeat salad sandwich and a cup of coffee for 15 cents. Another stand was said to be capitalizing on the crowd by charging 35 cents for a hamburger and a cup of coffee.

Many thought an explosion occurred due to a leak in the gas line or tank. It was said that Captain Johnson and the Foster boy had worked on the boat all day Saturday and that the boat had been put in the water and then taken back out twice. The Foster boy helped the Captain install the stove and adjust its stovepipe. They also did some work on the gas tank. The Don didn't get launched until 2:00 a.m. on the Sunday morning of the ill-fated cruise.

Some folks say if there had been an explosion, the 40 life preservers, said to be aboard, would have been scattered everywhere across the water and along the shorelines. Only one life preserver was found, and it had never been used. It was still folded just as it was when it came from the manufacturer.

If there had been an explosion, wouldn't someone have heard or seen something from out on the water or on the shore? Wouldn't the victims have been burnt? The first bodies recovered were thought to have burnt skin. Upon further examination, this proved to be a condition called "skin crawling," a natural occurrence when the skin has been exposed to the water for 24 hours or more.

The last body recovered was that of Adele Kawlaicze, 25, an employee of the Personal Finance Company in Rumford. She was found in the waters off Cape Small on July 14th, more than two weeks after the sinking.

Some folks held onto the belief that a German U-boat had sunk the Don and captured the 20 passengers that were never found. German submarines had been sighted in Casco Bay the month before, and war was raging in Europe. And in six months time, with the bombing of Pearl Harbor in December 1941, the United States was drawn into World War II.

Bernard Johnson was dragging for whiting out by Round Rock in 1967 when he pulled up his fishing net and found a pair of corroded opera glasses. The glasses had the initials L. S. and were known to have belonged to Lelia Sanders, private secretary of Paul Thurston, president of the Rumford Falls Trust Bank. On that same day another fisherman, Larry Bailey, was dragging alongside Bernard Johnson and hauled up the stern section of a boat that had flag gimbals like the one on the Don.

That afternoon when Bernard got in from fishing, he called the Rumford Bank and spoke with Thomas Dickson, who was now president of the Bank. Dickson, Paul Thurston and other Rumford officials came to Bailey Island, and Bernard took them out to Round Rock on his boat. Bernard let these folks know what he thought happened to the Don on June 29, 1941. He said Round Rock was a half-tide ledge that drops right off into 18 fathoms of water. Bernard said he believed the Don met its ruin at Round Rock. He figured the fog kept the party from getting to Monhegan that day, and they went ashore on Damariscove Island to picnic on chowder and wait for the fog to lift.

When the fog failed to lift, the Captain tried to feel his way back to Dyer's Cove in the dark. Captain Paul Johnson, a rumrunner in the past, knew the ocean at night and during bad weather as well as he did during daylight hours. He would have had no problem navigating after dark in the thick fog. Once he could feel the open water between Saddleback and Round Rock, he'd have a straight shot right up Quahog Bay to Dyer's Cove. Since there was absolutely no visibility and no bell on Round Rock at that time, Bernard was convinced that Captain Johnson ran the Don aground on treacherous Round Rock.

Raymond Gilliam happened to be fishing for sardines that night near Sisters Ledge, and he said he heard what sounded like a boat engine revving up, the way it would if someone were trying desperately to back off a ledge. Bernard said when a boat got hung up like that with groundswells building up in the bay, two or three waves would hit her, and she'd be gone.

Another local fisherman, Jim Harris, told Bernard Johnson about copper paint he kept finding on his ropes whenever he fished around Round Rock. (Copper paint is used on the bottoms of boats.) A grounding on Round Rock also explains why the first bodies were found in that area. An accident at night would also make us believe that Marie Rose Coulombe's watch stopped at 11:42 p.m. the night of the accident, not 11:42 a.m. on the morning of the cruise.

I guess no one will ever know for sure what happened to the Don and its 34 passengers.

The following fourteen victims are listed in the order their bodies were recovered:

Mrs. Dorcas Shand Kersey, 46, owner of Kersey's Millinery Shop and wife of Mr. John J. Kersey

Miss Bessie Strople, 39, clerk at Rumford Falls Trust Co.

Miss Ann Stisulis, 22, an Oxford Mill office employee

Miss Elizabeth Howard, 36, clerk at Rumford Falls Trust Co.

Miss Arlene Skolfield, 33, secretary to the Assistant Manager of Oxford Mill.

Earl Decker, 32, Assistant Personnel Manager at Oxford Mill, single

Miss Helen Decker, 30, Secretary to Attorney Ralph T. Parker

Miss Marie Rose Coulombe, 21, employed at Kersey's Millinery Shop

Captain Paul Johnson, 45, (not of the Harpswell Johnson's). His family came from Auburn, and he moved to Harpswell in 1931 to go lobstering.

Miss Ruth Hemingway, 38, Housekeeper for Dr. J. A. Green

Mrs. Carolyn Miller, 25, wife of Dr. Oscar Miller

Miss Leila Sanders, 48, private secretary to Paul Thurston at Rumford Falls Trust Co.

Mrs. Edith Coburn, 29, office employee of Harold McInnes Insurance (Edith did not appear to be married. She lived with her parents, and survivors did not include a husband.)

Miss Adele Kawlaicze, 25, employed at Personal Finance Co.

The victims below were never found:

Miss Mary Chapitas, 30, of Kersey's Millinery Shop

Miss Beatrice Roche, 20, of M.B.A. Insurance Agency

Miss Ramola Brundage of Reparessa, Calif, fiancee of Norman Foster

Norman Foster, 18, of Auburn, working for Captain Paul Johnson

Dr. Oscar Miller, 31, of Livermore Falls, Maine

Mr. John J Kersey, 44, owner Kersey's Jewelers

Albert Melanson, Sr., 48, Rumford Trust bank clerk, married

Albert Melanson, Jr., 18, Senior at Stephens High School

Robert Melanson, 15, son of Albert, Sr., student

Alban Melanson, 46, brother of Albert, Sr., clerk in JJ Dorions's Store, married

William Robertson, 18, Oxford Paper Mill

Dr. Robert Wishart, 27, dentist in Rumford, single

James Carey, Jr., 17, Stephens High School student

Albert Cormier, 37, until recently a clerk in Parent's Clothing Store, single

Edmund Cormier, 31, Rumford painter, single

Harry Hutchins, 19, Rumford Falls Power Co., single
Elliott Howard, 32, employed at Sunny Ridge Tea Room, single
Harold Elliott, 34, Eastern States Farmers' Exchange, single
Raymond Arsenault, 18, Stephens High School, senior
Oscar Bridgham, father of Carolyn Miller

Note: The above article was written by me and was printed in: Dis-cover Maine's –Western Lakes & Mountains magazine.

Author's Note:
I became very interested in this story after reading The Raven *by Peter Landesman. When* The Raven *first came out my husband Dennis bought me a copy for Mother's Day. He'd read the reviews and thought it might be something I'd like.*

I was fascinated with the story and couldn't believe it was based on an actual event and this was the first I'd ever heard of it! Although Peter Landesman chose to keep the book a work of fiction, he used a lot of the actual names of men from Bailey and Orr's Island.

It was hard for me to believe that a story about such a tragedy hadn't been passed down to our generation. I couldn't wait to talk to my mother and ask her about it. She said, "Oh yes, Janet, it was such a terrible thing! And nobody ever really knew the full story. I remember the day it happened as if it were yesterday though.

"It was a beautiful summer morning, and I had taken you and Gordon down to Cedar Island beach for the day. Gordon was seven and you were about two and a half. Cedar Island was your most favorite place to be. Gordon would go off and play with the other kids. But once you found your special round rock at the water's edge, you were happy to dive off it head first for as long as I'd stand there to pull you out and put you back up on your rock. As I've told you before, you had absolutely no fear of the water!

"Well, we ended up leaving the beach early that afternoon because it

*started clouding up and there was thunder rumbling off in the distance.
Along with everyone else who was still there, we gathered up our stuff and
started walking home before we got caught in the middle of the storm.*

"*It was the next day before we heard the news of the disappearance of
the Don. And then the fog came in and settled in for days. It was a terrible
thing when one of the fishermen brought in the first body. Then, almost
every day others were recovered. Up until that time everyone thought there
still might be a chance that the Don and its passengers had survived. Some
folks thought they could be stranded on one of the islands or something!
It was such an awful thing . . . all those young people dying and never
knowing why!*"

After I finished reading The Raven *and talking with several people
about it, my curiosity was really piqued! I did a lot of research at the local
libraries and viewed many reels of old microfilm photocopying anything
that had to do with the disappearance of the Don. The more information
I gathered, the more curious I became! Dennis and I even drove to Rumford one day. I visited the library while we were there, talked with a few
local ladies and took pictures of the Rumford Falls and Chisholm Park
where the Memorial Services for the victims was held on July 6, 1941.*

35
Brunswick Record Excerpts

Brunswick Record Excerpts—Bailey and Orr's Island News

February 8, 1923 – Sanford Prince who is taking a vacation at Tampa Beach, Florida writes home that he is having the time of his life. He will return home about March 1 to open his store, fish stand and coal pocket.

On account of the severe weather Herbert Shea, who has been working at his trade as a mason in Boston, returned home last Friday and remained here until conditions are such as to permit bricklaying.

The schools at the island were closed last Wednesday on account of a lack of fuel. We learn that our local coal dealer offered the school officials five tons of coal but would not screen it for them. As scarce as fuel has been on the island this winter it seems as though it was a foolish demand to ask for screened coal when there were a large number of private families that would have been more than pleased to accept coal in most any shape.

There are quite a large number of children confined to the house with a mild form of grip. Under the existing conditions, it would seem imperative that the schoolrooms be properly heated, so the pupils can attend to their studies in a comfortable manner.

A Ford Service Station will be opened at Black's Garage this week by Albert W. Black and Edward Richardson, under the firm name of Black and Richardson. Ford parts of all description will be handled and

Ford cars will be on sale.

Despite the hold up in town affairs and the stoppage of work on the roads, our highways are in good condition and many auto parties were at the island Sunday.

Clam diggers at the island are receiving the largest price for clams ever paid here. The clam grounds are about all covered with a thick coating of ice and there are only a few places where the diggers can work.

September 1, 1938 – Bailey Island News
Public Clambake on Beach to Feature Holiday at Bailey Island
Low Prices Will Prevail; Proceeds To Help Build Fire Dept. House

The Bailey Island Fire Department is planning another of its money-raising events for Labor Day, this time a public picnic and clambake on Mackerel Cove Beach.

The boys in the department see their way clear now to erecting soon a station for their two engines, and the proceeds from the clambake will be added to the funds already accumulated for this purpose. A plot of ground not far from the library, in a convenient location, has been made available, and the department hopes to have everything tidy before cold weather arrives.

The menu will be a typical old-time clambake, steamed clams, corn on the cob, crackers, butter, coffee, etc., with a price of 25 cents set for this portion of the meal. Lobsters and other foods will also be available extra.

The public is invited to attend, and the committee has arranged to have the bake at Library Hall if the weather is bad. Gus Johnson is in charge of the bake and food, and has delegated others to help him. Swimming and boat rides are to be available to round out the day and a program of sports of some sort will be arranged.

Phil Johnson, as chief of the department, has the worries of preparation on his shoulders, and others in charge of various items are: lobsters, Ed Black and George Johnson; clams, Leo Murray and Charles Leeman; corn, Charles Sinnett and Robert Gledhill. Murray and Leeman have arranged to have everyone available to turn on Sunday and dig clams for the event.

Tickets for the bake will be on sale at the beach. The boys point out that plenty of parking spaces will be available.

A dance in the evening at Library Hall has been arranged to round out the day.

September 8, 1938

The clambake at Bailey Island on Labor Day was more than a success. It served as a benediction to the summer season, and fine weather; a big crowd and the best of clams and lobsters made it memorable. The clambake was a benefit for the Bailey Island Fire Department, which is planning to erect a new fire station—the ground to be broken Thursday afternoon by Governor Lewis O Barrows.

January 5, 1939

Mr. and Mrs. Philip Freeman of Brunswick are receiving congratulations on the birth of a daughter: Mrs. Freeman was Selina Shea of Bailey Island.

Mr. and Mrs. Philip Freeman and two children are passing a month with Mrs. Freeman's mother, Hattie Shea.

August 1945

Earl Larrabee and Harold Shea recently brought in two tuna fish which were cut up and given to their friends at Garrison Beach on Bailey Island.

A Harpswell woman appeared in Portland Municipal Court on Monday for permitting gambling in a nickel slot machine at her place of business on Bailey Island. She was released on bail of $500 and the case was continued indefinitely.

July 18, 1946 – Front Page-
Two Tragic Deaths Occur Near Here
Man Drowns Off Orr's Island, Woman Burns in Truck

Two tragic deaths occurred as the result of accidents near Brunswick during the past week. A Bailey Island lobsterman, Arthur Leeman, was drowned when he fell from his boat early Monday morning. The second death took place Tuesday afternoon when Mrs. Mildred Wentworth of Oakland was trapped in the cab of a blazing fuel truck on the Brunswick-Freeport road.

Leeman was reaching for a mooring as he brought his fishing boat into Lowell's Cove at Orr's Island, shortly after midnight Sunday night. A companion, James Harris, was unable to sight Leeman after he had fallen into the water, and the body was not recovered until seven o'-clock on Monday morning as the result of dragging operations by Charles and Raymond Gilliam.

While he was standing on top of the cabin of the boat approaching the landing, a sudden lurch threw Leeman overboard and although firemen from the Bailey and Orr's Island departments searched throughout the night they could not recover the body.

Leeman was an Army veteran of three years, having been released from service last winter. He was born at Bailey Island on August 12, 1916, and was a lobsterman by trade.

He is survived by his parents, Mr. and Mrs. Charles Leeman of Bailey Island; three sisters, Mrs. Henry Snow of Orr's Island, Mrs. Winifred Sinnett of Bailey Island and Mrs. Ashbury Bailey of Wiscasset; and two brothers, Alton and Charles, Jr., of Bailey Island. Funeral Services were held at Bailey Island Church on Wednesday afternoon and interment was in the Bailey Island cemetery.

January 5, 1950

"Dairy Bar" at 31 Maine St., Brunswick is owned by B. Lacharite
Hrs are 6:00 AM—Midnight. Closed Sundays
"Ideal Lunch" at 141 Maine St., Brunswick
75 cent Specials:

#1 Soup, Fried Spring Chicken, Cranberry Sauce, Veg., FF's
#2 Soup, Fried Clams, Tartar Sauce, Veg., FF's,
#3 Soup, Grilled Pork Chops, Applesauce, Veg, FF's

May 11, 1950

New Bowdoin Drive-In with a 500 car capacity is opening for the summer. Other Theatres in the area are: Brunswick Drive-In, Cumberland, Pastime, Opera House in Bath and Nordica in Freeport.

January 25, 1951

Excellent drawing and article of the proposed construction job which will change the road to and from the islands.

(Note: My father was happy to get a job clearing and burning brush on Rte. 24 prior to the construction of the new road.)

April 26, 1951

Square Deal Restaurant is open for the season - Kay Shea and, Florence (Bunny) Leeman will be waiting on tables. Patricia Shea, call girl.

May 10, 1951

Janet Freeman, champion speller at the Orr's Island School was the winner of the Harpswell spelldown. She finished 4th in the District 14 Spelling Bee which was held last week in Freeport.

May 1951

Orchid Harbor—For Sale—Due to illness in the family, Mr. and Mrs. John Furth are selling the house with the 30 ft. Greenhouse attached. About 700 orchid plants are also offered for sale. The property was purchased in 1948 when the Furth's first came to Bailey Island. Since that time the 7 rooms and bath have been completely renovated. The Furth's moved the greenhouse and orchid plants from Staten Island in New York.

The house, which overlooks the bay, was built in 1883 and was previously known as the Robert York house. It is located at the North End of Bailey Island.

June 7, 1951

Pirate's Cove opened for the season.

June 1951

Children's Day Program at Church. The following young people participated in special Children's Day observance at the Union Church: Janet Freeman, Henry (Hank) Johnson, Nancy Johnson and Donna Leeman , Mrs. Ellis (Florence "Bunny") Leeman, Organist.

July 5, 1951

Forty-eight in attendance at Sunday School Outing at Cedar Beach.

August 2, 1951

August Dollar Days - "Dollar Days" at all the Brunswick stores!

Re-routing of Rte 24 changed due to building of NAS runway. Changes made to connect traffic at Cook's Corner instead of to Rte #123 (Harpswell Road).

August 1951

Captain Clayton Johnson and his son, Bernard brought in the first tuna of the season. In one day they "boated" 5 tuna dressed out and exceeded 2,000 lbs. A ton of tuna in one day!!

In 8 days of Tuna-Fishing, Captain Bill Munsey harpooned 3 tuna, for a total weight of 1,631 pounds.

Charles Harold Rogers harpooned a tuna Sunday halfway between Lumbo Ledge and Halfway Rock. It weighed approximately 550 lbs (405 dressed out). Roger's son, Don, accompanied him on the trip.

William Munsey boated a 350 lb (286 dressed) tuna Sunday. He ironed 3 tuna on Friday. Two were brought in at Bailey's Island, but the 3rd took off, buoy and all, and hasn't been seen since.

March 6, 1952

Joe and Kay Shea's 8 room house burned on Tuesday, March 4th in the early hours of the morning.

March 13, 1952

An unmistakable sign of spring was reported on Saturday. Seals were seen sunning themselves at the north end of Orr's Island.

Five Dead in Air Base Plane Crash!!

May 1, 1952

Joe and Kay Shea were given a variety shower at the Library Hall for their new home on Orr's Island.

May 1, 1952

Mossing started last week with John E. Sylvester, Jr. and William E. Sylvester, Jr. in charge of operations.

Note: Sea Moss is converted into a stabilizing agent for food, pharmaceuticals and industrial products.

May 1, 1952

Hermit Thrushes have come to the island.

May 8, 1952

Flickers and Blue Jays have arrived and strawberries are in blossom!

Members of migratory sets stopping off at Bailey Island last week include redwing blackbirds, fox sparrows, flickers and of course, robins.

Mayflowers have been reported picked.

Fishing News – Clayton Johnson caught a 40 lb. Halibut last week off Half-Way Rock. A day or two earlier, Elroy Doughty caught a 30-pounder.

36
My Scrapbook of the Islands

Island Dances – When Ethel Orr was sixteen she got her first as-signment to play for the Saturday night dances at Wilson's Hall on Orr's Island. Although Ethel's parents objected to her taking the ferry at night she convinced them that she'd be fine.

In those days, deep-sea fishing vessels anchored in Water Cove on Bailey Island and Lowell's Cove on Orr's Island. Often seen in Water Cove were the Albert W. Black with Capt. Harvey Black, the Eva Mildred with Capt. Fred Fides and the Moses B. Linscott with Capt. Charles York. Regular visitors in Lowell's Cove were the Vidie Brigham with Capt. Jake Brigham and the George H. Lubee with Capt. Maurice Lubee. When there was to be a dance in the evening, a flag was hoisted over the hall as a signal to the crews. All hands would rush to shore to attend the dance. Ethel also played the piano for the grammar school gradu-ation exercises at the Bailey Island Church in 1906. It was on that night that she met a young man who could sing and expertly play the violin. With their shared love of music, Ethel and Orrin Linwood Johnson be-came good friends, fell in love and got married.

Dances were sometimes held at the Seaside Hall over Ellis Orr's store, which later became Orrin Linscott's store and then the Lowell Cove Market on Orr's Island. Ethel Orr Johnson was the pianist at these dances. After the Red Men's Hall was completed in 1910 the dances were held there. Ethel Johnson again presided over the piano, while her husband Orrin played the violin, and their ten-year old son, Linwood, played the drums. Linwood was also very good at playing the bones. The three Johnsons made an effective three-piece orchestra.

I remember when . . . We had no dog food or cat food for our animals. They ate edible leftovers. There were very few paper products. Paper towels were nonexistent, toilet paper (used sparingly) no plastics, tissues (we used handkerchiefs); and there were very few magazines and books. We did get the catalogs from Sears & Roebuck and Montgomery Ward and the Portland newspaper on Sundays. If we ran out of Dr. Lyon's Tooth Powder we used either salt or Arm & Hammer Baking Soda to brush our teeth. I don't think there were many brands of tooth paste at that time, but I do remember when we got our first tube of Ipana Tooth Paste!

People said things like . . . She's a Tartar, Happy as a Pig in Shit, Gunning for Hunting, Brown as a Berry, She's a Keeper, Cunnin', Toe-head, Rum-Dum or Pie-Eyed, Dorey Plugs for Biscuits, Ass-end-to, Old Dingbat, Ungodly, Deader than a Doornail, Fell Head Over Tea Kettle, Punky Wood, Old Lard-Ass or Fat in the Can, Neat as a Pin, Full as a Tick and Chock Full.

Kids played games like . . . Leap Frog, Follow the Leader, Go in and Out the Window, Farmer in the Dell, Simon Says, Musical Chairs, London Bridges Falling Down, Red Light Green Light, Tag, Hide and Seek, Hopscotch, Marbles, Jump-rope.

Mackerel Traps – These traps consisted of a large net with corks all along the outer edge to hold the net up. After the net had set awhile, three or four men would pull the net up onto the boat with their hands. After the net was on board they'd dump the fish into the bottom of the boat until the net was empty. Once in awhile a shark would get caught in a mackerel trap and rip the net to shreds. The damaged net had to be brought into shore for repairs and all the fish would have escaped. Other nets were set farther out to catch herring and mackerel.

Drying Fish – To dry slack codfish or strip fish you would first clean out the codfish and cut off the head. After spreading the fish open, you'd lay it out flat on a wooden frame of light boards to dry in the sun. The fish had to be well salted or it would spoil.

Trawling – To go trawling, you'd have long lines with hooks that were spaced far apart. Usually you'd bait the trawl with old fish or cunners, before you left the shore. Some fishermen baited their hooks in the fish-house or outside in a field if it was a good day.

Trap-heads for Lobster Traps – These were knit by fishermen and their wives during the winter months when they couldn't get out to haul their traps. Most fishermen's homes had a hook mounted on the frame of a window with a view. Anyone could stand by a window knitting trap-heads and keep track of all the goings-on in the neighborhood at the same time.

Bailey Island Boats - Most fishermen were quick to tell you that boats made on Bailey Island were the best boats around! The well-built boats were rugged and had broad sterns and dependable engines. The canvas spray hoods that were tacked down on the sides of the boat near the bow served as a tent and kept off the ocean's spray. It also made a good place to sit to get away from the engine's exhaust fumes.

The Great Dolphin Catch - In 1822 a great school of dolphin appeared off Bailey Island. When the fishermen at the shore saw this they jumped into nine dories and drove the school of dolphin, like a herd of sheep, right into Mackerel Cove. The dolphin yielded 130 barrels of oil and sold for over $2,000. The money was divided amongst the fishermen that had caught them.

Steamboats – 1888 was the first year the steamboat came to Bailey Island. In those years it was moored at Orr's Island for the night, and it would leave there at 7:00 in the morning. About 20 minutes later it arrived at York's Landing at Lowell's Cove on Bailey Island. The steamboat delivered freight, coal, lumber, dry goods and mail, as well as passengers traveling to and from Portland.

With the arrival of the steamboat came the beginning of the tourist and cottage industry. In 1895 the steamboat landing was changed from York's Landing at Lowell's Cove to the Steamboat Wharf at Mackerel Cove.

On May 3, 1897 the 3-decked 117 foot Aucocisco was launched at Ferry Village in South Portland, Maine. She was referred to as the queen of the fleet and affectionately known as the Auco. Captain Charles B. Morrill of Orr's Island brought the Auco to Bailey Island four times a day from Memorial to Labor Day. Custom House Wharf in Portland was its destination, but the final trip of the day would find the Auco and Capt Morrill at rest on Orr's Island. Captain Morrill's beautiful home was just a short walk up the hill from where the Auco was moored for the night.

The old Auco was retired in 1952 and a second Aucocisco was built to take her place. It was little more than half as long as the first Auco and was driven by a diesel engine instead of steam. The old Auco's hoarse whistle that sounded like a young girl's husky voice was replaced with the undesirable shrill two-toned blast of the newer Aucocisco's whistle.

Tourist Industry – The Sea Shell Cottage that was built in 1883 was the first of many cottages to be built on Bailey Island. In the early 1900's land on the southeasterly part of Bailey Island was broken up and sold as cottage lots. Hotels and boarding houses sprung up shortly after and flourished. Livery businesses were started and their drivers with horse-drawn carriages would meet the steamboat each day and transport the tourists and their belongings to wherever they chose to spend a few weeks, months or the entire summer.

My Great-Grandfather Elisha Leeman had a livery business which he advertised in the 1904-05 edition of the Casco Bay Directory. He always dreaded those last days of summer when he'd bring the same folks he'd carried to their summer lodging in June back to the boat for their return home. All their luggage and trunks were twice as heavy from all the rocks they'd collected during their time on Bailey Island.

All Saints by the Sea Episcopal Chapel – Amy E. Blanchard and Ida Waugh organized the building of the summer chapel on Bailey Island that was completed in 1916. A chancel and sanctuary was added in 1920 due to the larger congregation. The little chapel on the road to Giant Stairs is still open during the summer months and has services on Sunday morning.

Cribstone Bridge – After much debate the construction of the Cribstone Bridge was finally authorized in 1924. F.W. Carlton of Woolwich, Maine signed a contract to build the bridge in 1926. The Knight Brothers Quarries in Pownal, Maine supplied the granite for the bridge. Ten thousand tons of granite slabs were loaded and floated by barge from Pownal. The barge traveled down the Cousin's River to the Royal River; to Yarmouth and then across Middle Bay around the tip of Harpswell Neck and up Harpswell Sound to the bridge site.

The bridge was finished in 1928 at an approximate cost of $139,000. The town of Harpswell contributed $22,000 toward its construction. A four-foot sidewalk was added to the east side of the bridge by the State Bridge Maintenance Force in 1951. The Cribstone Bridge, which is the only bridge of its kind, was added to the National Register of Historic Places on April 28, 1975. It was designated a National Historic Civil Engineering Landmark by the American Society of Civil Engineers in 1984.

Chapel of the Precious Blood – The first Catholic Church in the town of Harpswell opened its doors on July 30, 1949. The Bailey Island chapel was built in memory of Elizabeth Berry's deceased husband John Berry.

Harpswell Schools – Harpswell Islands School on Great Island was dedicated on August 11, 1957. The Bailey Island School was auctioned off in 1965, and George Stevens won the school with a bid of $1,554.

Bailey Island Businesses

Willow Cottage – Owned and operated by Mary Isabel (Black) Johnson and her husband, Walter Johnson from 1880-1890. Dr. Carl Jung once stayed at the Willow Cottage as well as Dr. Mann and other well-known psychoanalysts.

Ocean View Hotel – Walter Crafts built a cottage there first and then in 1899 added 15 rooms and a dining room. In 1900 he added eight more rooms. Then in 1902 he added another story and an additional seven rooms. The following year he added a veranda and another seven rooms. Ocean View Hotel was razed in 1963.

Springhouse Hotel – Merryman and Stover built the Springhouse Hotel. Some records show that in 1881 a spring water bottling service was started there. Possibly the lower level was the bottling area and the upper level served as a boarding house. In 1888 William Thomas Black was seven years old when he got his first job as an errand boy at the Springhouse Hotel. His duties included getting the mail and milk and running other errands of the same nature. This job was envied by most of his friends because it was about the only one open to a boy their age. Ethel Johnson and Charles Clary co-owned the springhouse from 1924-1926. The building was left vacant for many years and was then razed by Charles and Alton Leeman in February of 1935.

Robin Hood Inn – Dr. Eugene M. McCarty had it built as a religious retreat in the 1890's. The Inn got its name from Chief Ramegin, called Robin Hood by the English. Chief Ramegin had made his home on that section of the Island due to the pure waters that ran from the spring nearby. The spring was called the Robin Hood Spring and was known for its curative powers. U.S. Government vessels were known to put in from sea to secure their water supply from this spring.

The Robin Hood Inn was managed by Miss Julia Massey and operated as an Inn from 1903-1931. Their brochure described their vacation retreat as follows: "The inn rests on 12 acres of spruce and balsam with views of the restless sea from all areas. A sandy beach is in easy walking distance for swimming, boating, crabbing or digging clams. The pleasant rooms have good comfortable beds and are well-ventilated. Good food is well prepared and in ample quantity."

The Inn can be reached from Portland during July and August on the Steamboat that comes to the Island three times a day connecting with trains and steamboats from Boston and New York.

Driftwood Inn – Opened its doors as an Inn circa 1905 and was originally the Bigelow Cottage and Farmhouse on Little Harbor. Pleasant Place was added prior to 1920 and Surfside in 1930. A fire on September 23, 1947 took the original farmhouse.

The Driftwood Inn is the oldest Inn on Bailey Island. It has been in continuous operation and owned by the Conrad family for over 100 years. It sits on three acres of unexcelled ocean frontage. The rooms of the inn and the housekeeping cottages all offer panoramic views and cool sea breezes. You can watch the fishermen at work while relaxing in comfy chairs on the ocean-side porches, sunbathing on the private beach or swimming in the saltwater pool. Guests are served family style home cooked meals twice daily by a friendly staff in their ocean view dining room.

Rock Ovens – Joe Pitts and Hattie (Leeman) Shea began their business 1929-1930 when they started cooking seafood in rock ovens on the shore right next to the newly constructed Bailey-Orr's Island Bridge. It wasn't until 1940 that they were finally in a position to purchase the land on the most northerly end of Bailey Island, known as Garrison Point. Joe Pitts was then able to build the Rock Ovens Restaurant to ac-

Yale Shop

commodate their diners.

Yale Shop – Olive Mathieson owned the Yale Shop on the Steamboat Wharf Road and ran it as a small store and ice cream shop. The Yale Shop was formerly Stetson's Ice Cream Parlor.

Square Deal Restaurant – Opened in the early 1930's. Harpswell legalized beer sales in 1934 after six years of nationwide Prohibition. During this time Abby Clary and her husband Charlie had a beer parlor at Square Deal and Bert Rush built a platform for dancing across the road and provided live music. They had a lot of good times there until Harpswell families decided legalizing beer was causing too many problems, and at the next Town Meeting in 1935 they voted the town "dry". Abby Clary and Gertrude Leeman ran the restaurant together for 48 years. The Square Deal closed its doors in 1979.

Mackerel Cove Market – My mother and father Philip and Celina Freeman bought the Yale Shop from Olive Mathieson in the 1960's and ran it for several years as a grocery store with fresh meat, seafood and

Mum & Dad at Mackerel Cove Market

produce. A favorite of many of their customers was the haddock chowder my mother made and served most Fridays at the store. My parents enjoyed the business until my father's health failed and they were forced to sell in the late 60's. Shortly after the store was sold the buyer had the building razed. All that remains is a small garage and footprint of what once had been.

Jaquish Inn – Percy Allen built the Jaquish Inn and four to six light housekeeping cabins at the south end of Bailey Island circa 1930. In the early days Alice York cleaned cabins and was known as the cabin girl. Edna Johnson was in charge of the dining room of the inn. It was known for the great meals served there. Jean Doughty worked there when she was 13 years old. She served water, coffee and other beverages. The cabins remained open after the Inn closed in 1959.

Pirate's Cove Restaurant – Jerry and Helen Verville owned the restaurant in 1946. Russell and Joanne Lord bought Pirate's Cove in 1961 and renamed it Bridge Haven. The Lords sold Bridge Haven to Bruce Allen a few years later, and the Allens had it torn down in 1969.

Johnson's Market – In 1949 Phil Johnson opened his store across the road from Clayton and Winona Johnson's house on Bailey Island. Phil ran the store until his death in 1969. Harold Dayton bought the store and moved it out back of the post office where it sits to this day.

Bailey Island General Store (BIGS) –Harold Dayton built BIGS on the same site as the former Johnson's Market. The store was on the lower level of the two-story building and there were two apartments upstairs. The store has changed hands several times over the years but is presently owned by Teri (Johnson) Pontbriand. She has come back to the Island and her roots. Teri celebrated the first year anniversary of Grand Opening of BIGS on December 19, 2010. She'll retire from her job in May and we'll get to see more of her at the store.

In the meantime her sister Wendy Lefavor is holding down the fort. She's an imaginative and efficient cook and Pam Johnson (the girls' mother) is there to help and is usually tending the cash register. They are open for breakfast and lunch every day offering full breakfasts, sandwiches, subs, steak bombs, pastrami, lobster rolls (in season), great hamburgers, red hot dogs pizza and daily specials. A stop at BIGS is like coming back home after a long time away. It's a great place for folks to gather and visit for awhile.

Esso Gas Station – Ken and Polly Oliver moved to Bailey Island and opened an Esso filling station with two gas pumps and a garage in December of 1948. The station was brilliantly lighted for the first time the night before their opening day.

Cook's Restaurant – Maurice Cook built and opened Cook's Restaurant in 1955. Since that time the ownership has changed, but the food continues to be of the highest quality. Lobster, shrimp, scallops and shellfish are purchased right at their wharf to guarantee supreme freshness. Cook's has been selected one of the top ten seafood restaurants in New England for more than ten years in a row. Many special events take place at Cook's. Lobster bakes on Cook's Point, receptions, reunions, beer and wine dinners, fireworks in July, and tuna and sport fishing tournaments are held there every summer. The view from the dining room or Moby's Deck is spectacular! Norman Curtis Parent is the current proprietor.

Cook's Motel – Maurice Cook built Cook's Motel in 1957. It was Bailey Island's first motel. In recent years all eighteen rooms have been renovated and an in-ground pool is available. All rooms feature a private bath, cable TV, fridge and microwave. Guests can view breath-taking sunsets over Casco Bay from their deck. Open from Memorial Day weekend through Columbus Day.

Bailey Island Motel – Bruce and Joanne Allen built the five-unit Bailey Island Motel in 1959. In 1982 the Allens sold the Rock Ovens Restaurant and the Bailey Island Motel to Harold Dayton. Ralph ("Chip") H. Black, Jr. bought the Bailey Island Motel from Harold Dayton and has owned and operated the business for about 18 years. The motel is beautifully situated with sloping lawns, gardens and ocean-side Adirondack chairs. Guests can watch the sunrise, lobster fishermen at their work and enjoy the complimentary coffee and homemade muffins made fresh at the motel each morning. The motel has 11 clean quiet rooms, all with private bathrooms and cable TV.

Log Cabin Inn – Neal and Susan Allen Favreau bought the Log Cabin from John Wiseman of Lewiston, Maine in 1979. The Log Cabin was originally built as a summer home for Mr.Wiseman. Shortly after purchasing the Log Cabin Sue and Neal moved in with sons, Matt and Adam. In March of 2010 they celebrated their 30th year of business, 15 as a restaurant, and 15 as an Inn. After many years of additions and renovations they now have nine cozy unique suites, all with modern con-

S.J. Prince & Son – Salt Cod Cafe

veniences, a seaside swimming pool and an intimate dining room. They serve their guests a bountiful breakfast and an amazing array of appetizers, seafood entrees and deserts for dinner each night.

Salt Cod Cafe – Prince Specialty Seafood Products, Inc. – In 2004 Alison Prince established the Salt Cod Cafe/Prince Specialty Seafood Products, Inc. at Prince's Point on Orr's Island to continue the tradition of her great-great grandfather Sylvanus Cushing Prince. The Prince's believed in creating a market for local products, working with Maine companies and using as many Maine products and ingredients as possible to help support the local economy. The cafe is a great place for sandwiches, chowders, scones, homemade pies and pastries in season. Frozen chowders can be ordered and will be shipped year-round.

The Giant Stairs Seafood Grill – Chris and Heather Coffin are the present owners, and the restaurant is located right next to the Bailey Island Post Office. The Coffins serve breakfast, lunch and dinner, and their food is said to be the best home cooking on Bailey Island. They are open year-round, but their hours are limited on some days and on other days you might find them closed. Call ahead for hours – 207-833-5000

Land's End Gift Shop – This family run gift shop since 1959 has been a favorite destination for those who drive down Route 24 to the southern most tip of Bailey Island. It's the place to go for Maine-made items which include a Maine photo gallery, handmade crafts, pottery, jams, jellies and fudge, as well as thousands of items from around the world. Land's End Gift Shop has nearly 10,000 items in 7,000 square feet of shopping area on two floors. Bailey Island tee-shirts, sweatshirts, hats, mugs, souvenirs or anything LOBSTER can be found there.

Maine Lobsterman Statue – Elroy Johnson was chosen as the model for "The Maine Lobsterman" statue at Land's End on Bailey Island. Victor Kahill, was the Sculptor of the original statue made for the 1939-40 World's Fair. There are now two more: One on Maine Avenue in Washington DC and one in Portland, Maine. Elroy died in 1973 at age 79. He was a fisherman for sixty-five years.

Elroy Johnson's wife, Sadie, knit about 700 trap-heads in the winter of 1938 for Elroy's 275 traps. During the summer months Sadie fed hungry fishermen and tuna spectators at her restaurant, The Shanty Light, on the old Steamboat Wharf at Mackerel Cove.

A Few Notable People of Harpswell

Elijah Kellogg served as a minister of the Congregational Church (which now bears his name) in Harpswell from 1844-54 and served as Pastor until his death in 1901. He produced the Elm Island Series for young boys and many other popular adventure books for boys in the 1860's.

Harriet Beecher Stowe, known for her powerful book, <u>Uncle Tom's Cabin</u>, lived on Orr's Island when she wrote the <u>Pearl of Orr's Island</u>.

Robert Peter Tristram Coffin was born in Brunswick, Maine but his family moved to Prince's Point on Great Island when he was a boy. He won the Pulitzer Prize in 1934 for his book of verse entitled, <u>Strange Holiness</u>. In 1943 he told the story of his boyhood in Harpswell and Brunswick in <u>Lost Paradise</u>. Most of his works, prose or poetry, tell of Maine's virtues and her people.

Edna St. Vincent Millay became the first woman to win the Pulitzer Prize for poetry in the spring of 1923. She was awarded the prize for the best volume of verse published during the year, based on <u>The Ballad of the Harp-Weaver</u>, <u>A Few Figs From Thistles</u>, and eight sonnets published in <u>American Poetry, 1922, a Miscellany.</u>

It was said the first time Edna crossed the Orr's-Bailey Island Cribstone Bridge and looked eastward out to Ragged Island her exact words were, "I want that Island!" In 1933 Edna St. Vincent Millay was able to purchase the small house and all 85 acres of Ragged Island where she was to spend many glorious summers.

Edna was a good friend of a long-time Bailey Island summer resident, Esther (Tess) Adams. Tess said when Edna was receptive to company over on Ragged Island she would hang a flag that folks could see from Bailey Island.

James P. Gardner was widely known as the author of <u>Moneys of the World</u>, <u>Reminiscences of a Scottish Laddie</u>, <u>Peter Salt</u> and other short stories and poems inspired by Bailey Island. Mr. Gardner was a summer resident at the Island from 1920 until his death in the spring of 1950.

Dr. George Frederick Root (aka G. Fredrich Wurzel) was born August 30, 1820 and died August 6, 1895 at his summer home on Bailey Island. Dr. Root was a famed composer of many civil war songs, including <u>Just Before the Battle, Mother</u> and <u>Tramp! Tramp! Tramp!</u> George F. Root published over 500 pieces of music from 1848 until 1895.

Clara Louise Burnham was Dr. George F. Root's daughter. She was born in 1854 and she died at age 73 on Bailey Island. Clara was an accomplished author and wrote many books, a few of which I've listed here: Dr. Latimer: A Story of Casco Bay, The Opened Shutters, In Apple Blossom Time and Jewel.

Edmund "Rip" F. Black had just finished his junior year at the University of Maine when he entered the 1928 Summer Olympics in Amsterdam. He won the Bronze Medal in the Hammer Throwing event.

Admiral Robert E. Peary planted the American flag at the North Pole on April 6, 1909. His summer home at Eagle Island in Casco Bay is a Maine Historic Site.

References

Hancock County Courthouse, Ellsworth, Maine
Ellsworth City Hall, Ellsworth, Maine
St. Joseph's Catholic Church, Ellsworth, Maine
Ellsworth Public Library, Ellsworth, Maine
Town Office Records of Bar Harbor, Bristol, Georgetown and
    Harpswell, Maine
South Bristol-Rutherford Library, South Bristol, Maine
St. Charles of Borromeo Catholic Church, Woburn, Mass.
Woburn City Hall, Woburn, Mass.
Woburn Public Library, Woburn, Mass.
Pejepscot Historical Society, Brunswick, Maine
Maine State Library, Archives & Vital Records, Augusta, Maine
LDS Family History Library, Farmingdale, Maine
LDS Family History Library, Salt Lake City, Utah
National Archives for Military Records & Naturalizations,
    Waltham, Mass.
Cumberland County Registry of Deeds, Portland, Maine
Hawthorne Longfellow Library – Bowdoin College
    Books and Microfiche, Brunswick, Maine

Maine Historical Society, Portland, Maine
Curtis Memorial Library, Brunswick, Maine

Casco Bay Directory, Portland, Maine: Breeze Publishing Co.,
    (Crowley & Lunt, Publishers), 1901-02; 1920-22

Annual Town Reports of Harpswell, Maine

References

BOOKS ~
BAILEY ISLAND – Memories, Pictures & Lore
Nancy Orr Johnson Jensen 2003

The Evolution of Bailey Island, Beth Hill 1992

Charlie York: Maine Coast Fisherman, Harold B. Clifford,
    International Maine Publishing Co., Camden, Maine 1974

Coming of Age on Damariscove Island, Maine – 1910-1922
Alberta Poole's Island, by Carl R. Griffin
Alberta Poole Griffin, Author

Johnson Family History
Rev. Charles N. Sinnett

The Linscott Family in Maine
Compiled by Rev. Charles N. Sinnett, Brainerd, Minnesota
Updated by John E. Sylvester, Sr., Orr's Island, Maine

Black Family History
Prepared by Roy P. Webber II
Mountain Brook, Alabama
June 1994

NEWSPAPERS ~
Brunswick Record (Times-Record)
Lewiston Sun Journal
Portland SundayTelegram